INSIDERS'GUIDE®

OFF THE BEATEN PATH® SERIES

W9-AXE-177

Off the
SECOND EDITION
Beaten Path®

boston

A GUIDE TO UNIQUE PLACES

PATRICIA HARRIS
AND
DAVID LYON

INSIDERS'GUIDE®

GUILFORD, CONNECTICUT
AN IMPRINT OF THE GLOBE PEQUOT PRESS

The prices, rates, and hours listed in this guidebook
were confirmed at press time. We recommend,
however, that you call establishments to obtain
current information before traveling.

INSIDERS'GUIDE®

Text design by Linda Loiewski
Maps created by Equator Graphics © The Globe Pequot Press
Text illustrations by Carole Drong
Spot photography © Raymond Forbes/SuperStock

ISSN 1542–5967
ISBN 0-7627-3011-0

Manufactured in the United States of America
Second Edition/First Printing

For Dinah
who had to know
what was around each corner.

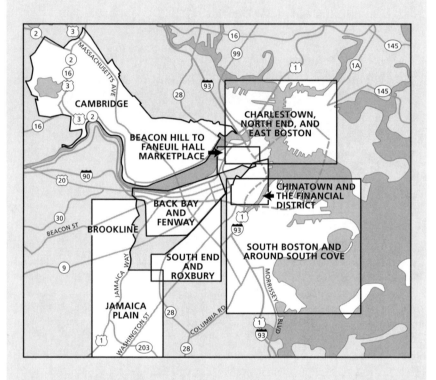

Contents

Introduction

Henry David Thoreau once wrote that "Whoever has been down to the end of Long Wharf and walked through Quincy Market has seen Boston." With due respect to the sage of Walden, he was missing a lot even in 1855, and the city has grown exponentially over the ensuing century and a half. While some visitors do seem to spend their whole time at Quincy Market, many expand their options by walking the justly famous Freedom Trail—the 3-mile-long path through Boston and, by extension, through America's early history. They might even take in one of Boston's art museums or concert halls or look for bargains at Filene's Basement.

Even those of us who live here rarely do more than scratch the surface of Boston. Exploring "off the beaten path" can be as simple as taking a turn off a well-traveled street to see what you can discover. That can be a lot of fun if you have the time. But even if your time is limited, this book will give you some starting points for exploring different Boston neighborhoods—from proper Beacon Hill to lace-curtain South Boston, from the jazzy digs of the South End and Roxbury to the Latin patter of East Boston and Jamaica Plain.

We're also assuming that if you're curious to leave the well-worn path, you're curious to know more about places you pass every day as well. Boston is a rich tapestry of buildings and places with quirky and personable tales. That's why you'll find some details on fine old houses wedged between clothing stores and cafes in Harvard Square, for example, and directions to let you enter some of Back Bay's mansions.

Some days you might just turn right instead of left as you follow a familiar route and find one of Boston's many hidden gems. But exploring off the beaten path can require some advance planning. Many lesser-known sites keep short or seasonal hours. In some cases you might have to make advance arrangements to see an attraction (which might explain why these places are off the beaten path). It can take some work to get to the lesser-known treasures. After you've climbed the Dorchester Monument for a stunning, king-of-the-hill view of Boston Harbor or sniffed a rare rose in the Kelleher Rose Garden in the Fenway, we leave it up to you whether to guard the secret of these overlooked places . . . or share them with your friends.

Getting Around

The Massachusetts Bay Transportation Authority (MBTA) operates more than 60 miles of subway and trolley lines in and around Boston. These trains are generally known as *"the T."* They operate from Monday through Saturday from

BOSTON TRAIN MAP

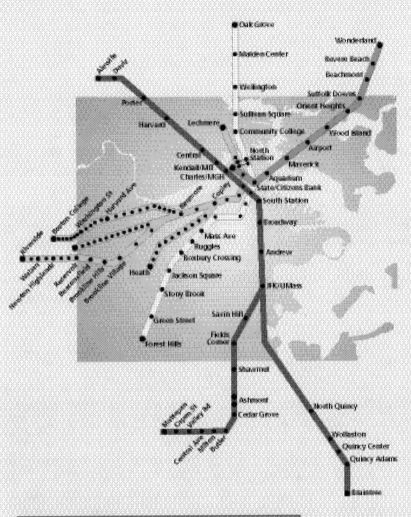

MBTA Trains Legend

▬▬▬ Red Line	● Terminal Station
▬▬▬ Blue Line	● Labeled Transit Stop
▬▬▬ Green Line	• Unlabeled Transit Stop
▬▬▬ Orange Line	●▬● Free Interchange

5:00 A.M. to 12:45 A.M., Sunday from 6:00 A.M. to 12:45 A.M., with late-night bus service paralleling the major lines until 2:00 A.M. on weekdays and 4:00 A.M. on weekends. Weekday service is officially every three to fifteen minutes, week-end service less frequent. One-way fares on the T are $1.25. The MBTA also operates more than 1,000 miles of *bus* lines serving primarily residential areas. Bus fare is 90 cents, exact change only.

If you intend to use public transport often, purchase a ***Visitor Passport.*** The Passport is valid for unlimited travel on T lines, buses, and inner-harbor ferries for one, three, or five days ($7.50/$18.00/$35.00). The passes are sold at South and North Stations, Airport Station, Downtown Crossing, and Alewife, as well as at the Boston Common and Prudential Center information centers. For information, call the MBTA at (617) 222–3200 or visit www.mbta.com.

If you're in an unfamiliar neighborhood after dark or if you get lost and need to return to a familiar landmark, take a cab. Boston is a civilized city, which means that you can flag down taxis on most streets. If the cabs are all occupied, head for the well-marked taxi stands located outside hotels. The ini-tial "drop fee" is $1.10 and all taxis are metered. Drivers expect a tip of 10 to 15 percent. The major taxi dispatch companies in Boston are ***Boston Cab*** (617–262–2227), ***Checker Taxi*** (617–536–7000), ***City Cab*** (617–536–5100), ***Metro Cab*** (617–242–8000), and ***Town Taxi*** (617–536–5000).

Fees, Prices, and Rates

Boston consistently ranks as one of the most expensive cities in the United States, just after Manhattan. This guide will give you a general idea of what you can expect to pay for meals: Under $20 per person is considered inexpensive; $20 to $45 is moderate; and more than $45 for a three-course meal is expen-sive. Lodging price guides are based on double rooms and do not include state and local taxes: Under $150 per night is inexpensive; $150 to $275 is moder-ate; more than $275 is expensive. Be sure to ask about special rates and pro-motions as well as such affiliation discounts as AAA or AARP.

Area Codes

Boston's original area code is 617, but new numbers are being issued using the 857 prefix as well. All numbers dialed in eastern Massachusetts must include the full ten digits.

Sources of Information

The best printed source for up-to-date information on what's happening in Boston is ***"Calendar,"*** a tabloid magazine published in the *Boston Globe* on Thursdays. The *Globe's* Web site, www.boston.com, provides *Calendar* as a searchable database. The **Boston Phoenix,** published on Fridays and available free from newspaper racks, remains a stronger, if less inclusive, source of information about clubs and bars.

Free visitor information kits may be obtained from the **Greater Boston Convention and Visitors Bureau,** 2 Copley Place, Suite 105, Boston, MA 02116–6501; (617) 536–4100 or (888) 733–2678; www.bostonUSA.com. Advance information on Cambridge is available from the **Cambridge Office for Tourism,** 18 Brattle Street, Cambridge, MA 02138; (617) 441–2884 or (800) 862–5678; www.cambridge-usa.org.

For maps and other information once you've arrived, stop at the **visitor information centers** at 146 Tremont Street on the Boston Common, at Center Court in the Prudential Center (800 Boylston Street), or at the kiosk near the subway entrance in Harvard Square, Cambridge.

For restaurant reviews, performing arts listings, and downloadable maps, visit the Ticketmaster-owned Web site, Boston.citysearch.com. Similar maps are also available on Expedia.com. For information on public art in the city, visit the Greater Boston Arts Public Art Web site at www.wgbh.org/wgbh/pages/bostonarts/publicart.

Tour Groups and Organizers

Boston is amply endowed with tour buses and trolleys to take you to the usual sites. But to leave the crowds behind, look into these tours, where knowledgeable guides help you focus on the road less traveled.

Boston Park Rangers lead a variety of free programs that help uncover the secrets of the city's parks, including stargazing at the Arnold Arboretum, bird watching in the Back Bay Fens, and an ambitious full-day, 7-mile hike of the Emerald Necklace. Call (617) 635–7383.

National Park Service Walking Tours. Ranger-led tours are the classic introduction to historic Boston. Free daily tours depart from the Boston National Park Visitor Center at State and Devonshire Streets. Call (617) 242–5689 for details.

Historic Neighborhoods Foundation. Don't be misled by the name. This organization often leads behind-the-scenes tours of some of Boston's newest developments. Rates vary. Call (617) 426–1885 for schedule.

Boston by Foot. Regularly scheduled walks include Beacon Hill, the Back Bay, the North End, the Waterfront, and Boston Underground. "Tours of the Month" explore other neighborhoods or themes. The fee is $9.00. Walks are offered from May through October. Call (617) 367–3766 or visit www.boston byfoot.com.

Boston Spirits. This tour of purportedly haunted locales takes place only in the evening so that walkers will have a better chance to see the spirits lurking in the shadows. Tours depart from the visitor center on Boston Common. Fee is $14. Call (781) 235–7149 for dates and to make reservations.

WalkBoston. Enthusiastic and knowledgeable volunteers lead visitors through overlooked neighborhoods and explore such topics as the geology of Boston. Call (617) 367–9255 or visit www.walkboston.org.

Boston Bike Tours. Boston's relatively flat terrain and compact size make it a natural for touring by bike. Two-hour tours Monday through Saturday might cover Harvard Square, the Freedom Trail, or several Boston neighborhoods. More ambitious four-hour Sunday tours include the Emerald Necklace, South Boston, and a combined Freedom Trail/Harvard Square outing. Tours operate from mid-April to mid-October. Fees ($20–$25) include bicycle and helmet. Visit www.bostonbiketours.com or call (617) 308–5902.

Sunday Morning City Skate. A chance to skate the streets of the city at a time when the traffic is light. Sponsored by the Inline Club of Boston. The group assembles from May through October at 10:15 A.M. at JFK Park (corner of Memorial Drive and JFK Street in Cambridge). Visit www.sk8net.com or call (781) 932–5457 for the skating event hot line.

Old Town Trolley Tours. In addition to standard city tours with unlimited reboarding, Old Town offers a number of specialty tours throughout the year, such as the "Chocolate Tour," "Ghosts and Gravestones," "JFK's Boston," and "Holiday Lights." Call (617) 482–1279 or visit www.trolleytours.com/boston.htm.

Beacon Hill to Faneuil Hall Marketplace

Boston's leading tourist attraction isn't any individual building, park, or institution—it is the imaginary connection among a handful of historic spots. This connection is known as the Freedom Trail. Thousands of visitors "connect the dots" and travel the Freedom Trail every year, yet in their purposeful pursuit of history, they often fail to step a few yards off this well-beaten path to see some equally remarkable aspects of Boston.

This chapter begins with Beacon Hill and parallels the Freedom Trail (more or less) downhill through the historic Downtown district to Faneuil Hall Marketplace. Those of us who live in this part of the city often take it for granted. But few places like Beacon Hill—an entire urban neighborhood solidly rooted in the early nineteenth century—exist in the United States. And even though much of Boston's Downtown arose from the ashes of the 1872 fire, large portions still reflect a city that was already old when the country was new.

Beacon Hill

Beacon Hill has an image as the most exclusive of Boston enclaves, a preserve of old families with old money who have occupied its heights since the area was first developed in the late 1790s. And that image is half right.

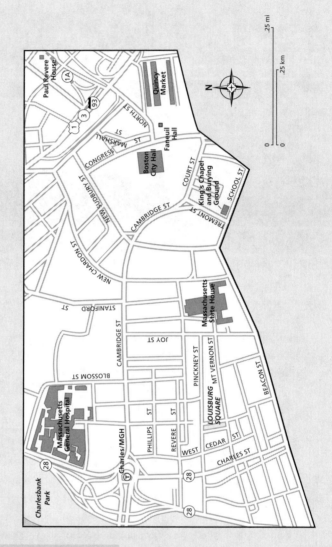

One of the developers of Beacon Hill was architect Charles Bulfinch, who was instrumental in establishing a building code for the district that not only promoted his design style but also produced one of the most architecturally coherent neighborhoods in the country. Built by the moneyed class for the moneyed class, one side of Beacon Hill

where JFK hung his hat (or his ballot)

While John F. Kennedy served the 11th District in the U.S. Congress (beginning in 1946), he lived at the Bellevue Hotel on Beacon Hill, now condominiums. It remained his legal voting address until his death.

developed into the natural den of the Boston Brahmin, as described by Oliver Wendell Holmes as a "harmless, inoffensive, untitled aristocracy" with their "houses by Bulfinch, their monopoly on Beacon Street, their ancestral portraits and Chinese porcelains, humanitarianism, Unitarian faith in the march of the mind, Yankee shrewdness, and New England exclusiveness."

But there's literally another side to Beacon Hill. While the south slope, closest to Boston Common, developed as an exclusive community, the north

Painless History

Massachusetts General Hospital frequently makes medical history, but one of its oldest accomplishments remains one of the most significant: general anesthesia. From the Charles/MGH T stop, turn right as you exit the turnstiles to reach Cambridge Street. A few blocks up on the left, one street after the main entrance to the Massachusetts General Hospital, is North Anderson Street. At the end of the block, another gate leads to the oldest part of the hospital complex, the **Bulfinch Pavilion.** Designed by Charles Bulfinch and constructed from drawings by Alexander Parris (architect of Quincy Market) between 1818 and 1823, the structure stands embedded in later alterations and additions. But in the fourth-floor operating theater, lit by an overhead glass dome, Dr. John Warren conducted the world's first public demonstration of surgery under general anesthesia in 1846. Using a device he had invented, dentist William Thomas Green Morton administered ether to Gilbert Abbot, and Warren removed a tumor from Abbot's jaw. The response from the medical community was nothing short of sensational. "We have conquered pain!" Warren announced. Until the use of ether, surgery had always been a last resort because the trauma of operating was often as much a risk to the patient as the condition being treated. The operating amphitheater is still used for academic conferences and lectures, but otherwise the **Ether Dome** and its small museum dedicated to the historic event are open to visitors Monday through Friday from 1:00 to 3:00 P.M. Free admission. Call (617) 726–8540.

slope, which overlooked the harbor in earlier times, served as the toehold for wave after wave of immigrants, beginning with Boston's free African-American community.

This walking tour of Beacon Hill winds up and down its undeniably picturesque streets—on both sides of the hill—introducing you to a whole range of characters who have lived on the heights. The best place to begin is at the Charles/MGH stop on the T's Red Line.

Turn left when you exit the subway to reach **Charles Street,** where the antiques dealers claim that their profession began in the United States. It has been observed that when the family fortunes of the original Brahmins dwindled, their progeny kept chèvre on the table and Chassagne-Montrachet in the refrigerator by slowly deaccessioning the family knickknacks, china, and furniture. Today's area antiques shops often specialize in New England, China trade, Asian, or European antiques, but few of the goods, we suspect, ever graced the front parlors of Beacon Hill. Nonetheless, Charles Street is immensely popular for strolling, shopping, and stopping for a drink or a bite at its many restaurants, bars, and cafes. If you follow our suggestions for walking Beacon Hill, reveling in the Federal atmosphere of a neighborhood where visible changes to your house require the neighborly equivalent of a Papal dispensation, you'll return several times to Charles Street—maybe just in time for a needed libation.

Poet Robert Lowell referred to his childhood home as sitting on Beacon Hill's "unbuttoned North Slope," a wonderfully evocative indication that it was not, in those days, the part of the Hill occupied by the socially prominent. If you take a left from Charles Street onto Revere Street, you'll walk right past the home in question (**91 Revere Street**). Part of Revere Street's appeal is the group of several tiny cul-de-sacs that extend from the north side of the street. If you keep walking up Revere until the street finally flattens out, you'll see **Rollins Place** on the left. In this dense tunnel of Federal brickwork, a white portico beckons at the end of the alley—as if a Southern plantation manse were being held captive by Boston bricks. But the portico is only a trick of the eye, an architectural jest that disguises a 20-foot drop to Phillips Street below.

To visit one of the premier sites in Boston's Jewish history, turn left on Garden Street and left again on Phillips Street. The **Vilna Shul** at 14 Phillips Street is the last of more than fifty Jewish worship centers that once flourished in central Boston. Its congregation of Jews from Vilna, Lithuania, was founded in 1814. They built this structure in 1919 in a splendid marriage of medieval European synagogue and New England meetinghouse. The congregation dwindled over the years to a single member in 1985, and in 1990 the structure was purchased by the Boston Center for Jewish Heritage. Although the building will be undergoing restoration for many years, it is open to visitors Sunday 1:00 to 3:00 P.M. from Passover through Thanksgiving. Free admission. Call (781) 416–1881.

The houses along Phillips Street are not the Hill's showiest,

but this remains a strong residential neighborhood, brightened by such fine touches as Phillips Street Park, directly across from Vilna Shul. If you continue down the street, you'll come to the *Lewis Hayden House* at 66 Phillips Street, perhaps the single most significant abolitionist site in Boston. Himself a fugitive slave, Hayden sheltered many a passenger on the Underground Railroad. He fiercely resisted all attempts to search his house, and he routinely threatened to blow up the property with the kegs of gunpowder in the basement if a slave-catcher stepped across the threshold. A plaque on the building celebrates Hayden as "fugitive slave, leading abolitionist, Prince Hall Mason, rescuer of Shadrach, member of the General Assembly, messenger to the Secretary of State."

To continue exploring Beacon Hill, walk down Phillips to West Cedar Street, turn left and cross Revere Street, and turn left onto *Pinckney Street,* the former dividing line between black and white, rich and poor on Beacon Hill. John J. Smith broke that color line in 1878 when he purchased the house at *86 Pinckney* on the "white" side. The colors that most interest Beacon Hill residents today, however, are blossoms that will thrive on the shady streets and in their hidden back gardens. On a facing corner to the John J. Smith House, *Rouvalis Flowers* at 40 West Cedar supplies not only those blooms but an array of garden ornaments, decorative pots, and some antiques. It's open Monday through Saturday 9:00 A.M. to 6:00 P.M. Call (617) 720–2266.

Louisburg Square, one of the most beautiful enclaves of Beacon Hill, is a long block uphill. The tall mansion at *85 Pinckney Street,* at the end of the square,

The Lettered Lady on Louisburg Square

As a child, **Louisa May Alcott** lived at 20 Pinckney Street in rooms rented by her ne'er-do-well philosopher father, Bronson Alcott, before the family moved out to Concord. With her reputation and fortunes secure, in the 1880s Louisa purchased a Beacon Hill home at 10 Louisburg Square for her family. Her father died there in 1888, shortly before Louisa herself passed on, possibly from mercury poisoning received as treatment for typhoid she contracted as a Civil War nurse.

hardlypublic

Louisburg Square is the last remaining private square in the city of Boston.

is the site of one of Beacon Hill's most scandalous crimes, the so-called Debutante Murder. In 1962 a pregnant Suzanne Clift, socialite niece of actor Montgomery Clift, shot her boyfriend, Pierro Brentani, allegedly because he would not marry her. (Suzanne Clift served time in a mental-health facility, then married and moved to Texas, disappearing from public view after 1970.)

As one of the oldest streets on Beacon Hill (portions predate the development of the Hill in the 1790s), Pinckney Street offers fascinating juxtapositions of elegant town houses with modest apartment buildings and a handful of small wooden houses. The *Glapion Middleton House* (5 Pinckney Street) was built in 1791 by George Middleton, a black coachman and soldier in the Revolutionary War, and Louis Glapion, a mulatto barber. It is the oldest residential structure on Beacon Hill, and one of the least altered.

Pinckney ends at Joy Street. To understand something of the history of African-American Boston, turn left and walk down Joy to visit the *African Meeting House* at 8 Smith Court, home of the *Museum of Afro-American History.* Boston's substantial free black community (Massachusetts outlawed slavery in 1783) built this church in 1806 to rival segregated white churches of the area, and the meetinghouse became a lightning rod for abolitionists. William Lloyd Garrison founded the influential New England Anti-Slavery Society here in 1832.

The Museum of Afro-American History occupies the meetinghouse and the adjacent *Abiel Smith School,* the first black private school in Boston. The school was founded in 1835 and closed in 1855, when the Massachusetts Legislature mandated racial integration of the public schools. It is open Monday through Saturday 10:00 A.M. to 4:00 P.M., Sunday 10:00 A.M. to 4:00 P.M. in summer. Suggested donation $5.00. Call (617) 725–0022.

Mine Eyes Have Seen the Glory

Julia Ward Howe lived at 13 Chestnut Street at the outbreak of the Civil War. It was here that she wrote the verses to "The Battle Hymn of the Republic." Howe was an abolitionist, suffragist, and tireless reformer who initiated Mother's Day to demonstrate for peace. The house was designed in 1806 by Charles Bulfinch for Hepzibah Swan, an investor in the development of Beacon Hill who might be considered Boston's first feminist. It was one of three adjoining houses that Swan presented to her daughters as wedding presents.

Many nearby householders willingly sheltered fugitive slaves en route to freedom in Canada. The rabbit warren of mews and alleys on Beacon Hill foiled even the most relentless slavecatchers. At the end of Smith Court, **Holmes Alley** was one of the many escape routes for fugitives.

After this sojourn into the heroic side of Beacon Hill,

notacting

Actor Edwin Booth was living at 29A Chestnut Street when he received the news that his brother John Wilkes Booth had assassinated Abraham Lincoln. He canceled his last performance and left town. His residence, the oldest house built by Mount Vernon proprietors, is known for its purple windowpanes.

retrace your steps up Joy Street to Mount Vernon Street, which Henry James declared "the most civilized street in America." When landscape designer and author Rose Standish Nichols died in 1960, her will established the **Nichols House Museum** at 55 Mount Vernon Street to give visitors without family connections or business ties the chance to appreciate a Beacon Hill home. Rose Nichols never married, but she was an ardent political activist and ran her own version of an artistic salon in this house designed by Charles Bulfinch and modified around 1830. Take the opportunity to peer inside not just a home, but the idiosyncratic life of a true Beacon Hill character as well. The museum is open May through October, Tuesday through Saturday noon to 4:00 P.M.; November through April, Thursday, Friday, and Saturday noon to 4:00 P.M.; closed January. Admission is $5.00. Call (617) 227–6993.

The march down Mount Vernon Street passes an array of famous mansions on the right and more modest homes on the left. Sculptor Anne Whitney (1821–1915) kept her studio at **92 Mount Vernon** Street for two decades. Her most visible Boston works are the statue of Samuel Adams outside Faneuil Hall and the heroic figure of Leif Eriksson on Commonwealth Avenue mall. If you turn left onto

Beacon Hill Classic Doorway

everybody knows your name

The television sitcom *Cheers!*, set at the site of the Bull & Finch Tavern at 84 Beacon Street, made its debut in 1982. It bore a striking conceptual resemblance to a locally produced sitcom, *Park Street Under*, that ran on Channel 5 a few years earlier.

Charles Street and left again on Beacon Street, you'll be passing the most coveted Beacon Hill mansions of all—those that face Boston Common.

The **William Hickling Prescott House** at 55 Beacon Street, a Federal-style house built for a wealthy merchant in 1808, was designed by Asher Benjamin. Benjamin was Charles Bulfinch's contemporary and (at least in the minds of some architectural historians) his rival for grace and style. Prescott, the historian famous for his accounts of the Spanish conquests of Peru and Mexico, dwelled here from 1845 to 1869. Prescott had lost his vision in one eye during a food fight at Harvard. He dealt with his impaired vision by using the "noctograph" that is displayed on his former desk. The grooved surface allowed him to write in straight lines across the page. In the 1930s the Massachusetts Society of Colonial Dames rescued the house from conversion to a boarding house. Three different eras are represented, including the Federal period of the first occupants, the high Victorian style of Prescott's era, and one of the earliest Colonial Revival rooms in the U.S. (circa 1870). The Dames also display a variety of period costumes. Open Wednesday, Thursday, and Saturday noon to 4:00 P.M. Admission $4.00. Call (617) 742–3190.

Given the propriety of Beacon Street, it's surprising that a tinge of scandal still clings to the **Parkman House** at number 33 a century and a half after one of Boston's most sensational murders. In November 1849 Harvard professor Dr. John Webster apparently murdered his fellow socialite, Dr. George Parkman,

Flanked by Conscience

Legislators in the Massachusetts State House are not likely to forget about freedom of religion, not with **statues of early religious dissenters** Anne Hutchinson and Mary Dyer on the front lawn. A respected midwife and wife of an established merchant, Hutchinson was banished from Boston in 1638 for heresy because her beliefs contradicted the religious authority of Puritan ministers. (She believed in a direct personal connection to God.) Five years later she was killed in the wilderness of New Netherland, now New York, by Hudson River Indians. Mary Dyer, whose Quaker faith also dispensed with the need for clergy, refused to acknowledge the ban on Quakerism imposed by Boston's theocracy. She was banished twice from the city, and when she came back a second time, she was hanged on Boston Common in 1660.

who had donated the land for Harvard Medical School (now the site of Massachusetts General Hospital). As Harvard president Jared Sparks testified, "[Harvard] professors do not often commit murder," which only fed the scandal. Judge Lemuel Shaw, a Parkman relative, condemned Webster to hang, encouraging the newspapers to accuse the family of closing ranks. Parkman's son, daughter, and widow retreated to this house, and the son, George Francis Parkman, lived here in seclusion until he died in 1908. The house was willed to the city and is used occasionally for receptions and conferences.

heretics and other free thinkers

In the mid-1630s, "heretic" Anne Hutchinson lived across from Governor John Winthrop, where The Boston Globe Store now stands on the corner of School and Washington streets. The present building housed the publishing house of Ticknor and Fields, publishers of Emerson and Thoreau, among others.

As you continue walking toward the highest point in downtown Boston, you'll pass the State House and the Shaw Memorial. The eight-story granite and brick building at 14 Beacon Street is the *Congregationalist House,* but it also served as the fictional home of the law firm Cage & Fish (on the seventh floor) on the Fox television show Ally McBeal. Although the show was filmed elsewhere, it seems fitting that some of television's more colorful characters would work on Beacon Hill.

Downtown

The heart of downtown Boston links Beacon Hill to Government Center and Faneuil Hall Marketplace. If you continue following Beacon Street, it wraps around the peak of the hill and plunges down to Tremont Street. When it crosses Tremont, the name changes to School Street. (If you've skipped Beacon Hill, take the Red or Green Line subway to Park Street Station and follow Tremont to School Street.) Right on the corner stands the historic *Parker House,* the

Hidden Gardens of Beacon Hill

Whenever we stroll on Beacon Hill, we find it intriguing to catch just a glimpse of color behind a wall or around the corner of a house. The Beacon Hill Garden Club understands that curiosity and has sponsored the *Hidden Gardens of Beacon Hill* tour on the third Thursday of May since 1929. The self-guided walking tour lets you enter the gardens that flourish in the tiny backyards behind the big houses. Call (617) 227–4392.

Praise the Sound

Every Tuesday at 12:15 P.M., King's Chapel at the corner of School and Tremont Streets swells with the sound of *musical recitals,* many of them employing the majestic Charles Fisk organ. The series has become something of a Boston tradition since the first recital at 11:00 A.M. on Tuesday, January 10, 1786. (There have been lapses.) Suggested donation $2.00. Call (617) 227–2155.

oldest continuously operating hotel in America and birthplace of both the Parker House roll and Boston cream pie. In the nineteenth century the Parker House was a magnet for celebrities, and America's literary elite—Ralph Waldo Emerson, Henry Wadsworth Longfellow, James Russell Lowell—met here every Saturday. In the twentieth century Ho Chi Minh was a busboy here, Malcolm Little (later Malcolm X) a waiter. A few display cases in the sumptuous lobby commemorate illustrious visitors and special dinners.

Across School Street, a colorful sidewalk mosaic in front of Old City Hall marks the site of the *Boston Latin School,* established in 1635 as the first public school in the country. The statue of *Benjamin Franklin,* erected in 1856, was the city's first public statue. Sculptor Richard Saltonstall Greenough modeled the statue's fur-lined coat on one of Franklin's suits in the collection of the Massachusetts Historical Society. The other statue celebrates *Josiah Quincy,* Boston's second mayor. Quincy literally cleaned up the city by building Quincy Market to replace the muddy wharves of Dock Square, establishing the first municipal garbage pickup, and laying the city's first extensive sewer lines—all in the 1820s.

At Washington Street, jog right to the head of Milk Street, where the 1 Milk Street office building has swallowed up Benjamin Franklin's birthplace at 17 Milk Street. Across Milk Street, in the basement of the Old South Meeting House, *Antiquarian Books of Boston* provides a tangible (and portable) taste of the past. It's open Sunday

smallbeer

Be sure to duck at the doorway when you step down into the accurately named *Littlest Bar* below Cafe Marliave at 47 Province Street. Hardly bigger than a railroad car, the bar has a maximum legal occupancy of thirty-eight. It also has Guinness on draft. Call (617) 523–9766.

to Thursday 10:00 A.M. to 6:00 P.M., Friday 10:00 A.M. to 2:00 P.M. (closed Saturday). Continue down Milk Street and turn left on Devonshire Street, a canyon lined by outstanding Art Deco office buildings, to State Street. Walk down State and turn left on Congress to reach one of the most visited places in Boston (indeed, in the country), Faneuil Hall.

Here's the Scoop

At the corner of State and Congress Streets, make a 100-foot detour toward Post Office Square to one of Boston's tastiest traditions, the coffee shop **Brigham's** at 50 Congress Street. Brigham's created a special ice cream flavor in honor of the city's massive construction project. "Big Dig" is a rich vanilla ice cream packed with gobs of brownie, chunks of chocolate, and swirls of caramel. And the shop still makes ice cream sodas. This Brigham's is open Monday through Friday 6:30 A.M. to 5:30 P.M., closed weekends. Call (617) 523-9372.

Faneuil Hall Marketplace

In Boston's first decade, the town docks were on Bendell's Cove, where the waves lapped at the edges of what is now Congress Street in front of Faneuil Hall. (If you've skipped the earlier parts of this chapter, you can get to this area quickly on the Green or Orange Lines to the Haymarket T Station.) The pavement at the foot of the **Samuel Adams statue** (sculpted by Anne Whitney of Beacon Hill) was inscribed by artist Ross Miller with an outline of the original Shawmut Peninsula shoreline. Millions of feet have worn down Miller's work, so you'll have to look closely to see his fanciful imprints of ropes, codfish, seashells, clams, and kelp, reminders that this spot was once under water.

Most visitors climb to the second floor of Faneuil Hall to see the auditorium that earned the building its nickname as the "cradle of liberty," then head to the shops of the surrounding marketplace. Few continue up the stairs to the fourth floor to see the **Museum of the Ancient and Honorable Artillery,** the oldest chartered military organization in the western hemisphere. Since its founding in 1638, members have served in every conflict from early Colonial Indian wars to twenty-first century operations in Afghanistan and Iraq. The headquarters and armory have been in Faneuil Hall since 1746 and, unlike much of the building, this attic room remains original to

cue the shortstop

All-Star Red Sox shortstop Nomar Garciaparra likes to hang out at **Rack Billiards Club** near Faneuil Hall, where table no. 22 is his favorite. Of the twenty-two beige-felted tables, all are regulation except for the third one on the right as you enter. It's a foot shorter than the others to provide adequate cue room around an immovable pillar. The Rack is at 20 Clinton Street. Call (617) 725-1051.

Charles Bulfinch's 1805 reconstruction. Mementos include shells fired in the Spanish-American War, a cannonball from the Battle of Bunker Hill, and Union

Never Forget

"They came first for the Communists and I didn't speak up because I wasn't a Communist. They came for the Jews and I didn't speak up because I wasn't a Jew. They came for the Catholics and I didn't speak up because I was Protestant. Then they came for me, and by that time there was no one left to speak up." In words attributed to Lutheran pastor Martin Niemoeller, a stone slab at one end of the **Holocaust Memorial** captures one of the principal, if horrific, lessons of the twentieth century: the individual's moral responsibility to resist evil. Four glass towers, etched with numbers, stand like ghostly chimneys of the extermination camps, while engraved narratives tell of individual horrors, acts of heroism, and simple decency.

and Confederate bullets. One small case is devoted to John F. Kennedy's application for membership in October of 1955. (He was elected to the Artillery in April of 1956.) The museum is open Monday through Friday 9:00 A.M. to 3:30 P.M. Free admission. Call (617) 227–1638.

Disregard, if you can, the McDonald's on the corner of the **Blackstone Block** across North Street from Faneuil Hall. This network of narrow, winding streets has withstood change since the 1600s, and if you squint hard, you can almost imagine yourself in the Boston of Puritan theocrat Cotton Mather. Blackstone Street, the northeast boundary of the block, was the original butchers' street, with a creek running past to dispose of waste. It is still a street of butchers, though many of them today follow the strict dietary laws of Islam. Marsh Lane, Salt Lane, Creek Lane, Scott Alley (perhaps the narrowest alley in Boston), and Marshall Street all flow into Creek Square, the center of the block, where the history of the area is encapsulated on information panels.

On one corner of Creek Square, the **Boston Stone** is embedded at ground level at 9 Marshall Street. Painter Thomas Child brought the spherical grind-

Old-Time Flavors

Union Oyster House at 41 Union Street and **Durgin-Park Restaurant** in South Market of Faneuil Hall Marketplace both opened in the 1820s—proving that good New England–style cooking has staying power. Union Oyster's semicircular bar dates from its opening and remains one of the best places in the city for bivalves on the half shell. Be sure to make a reservation, though, if you're planning a full meal. At Durgin-Park, once you've waited your turn in line, grab a seat at a communal table for immense slabs of prime rib, or for baked beans and franks with Yankee (molasses-sweetened) cornbread. Union Oyster House is moderate to expensive; call (617) 227–2750. Durgin-Park is inexpensive to moderate; call (617) 227–2038.

stone from England around 1701 to grind his pigments, making it perhaps Boston's oldest industrial artifact. Popular lore holds (incorrectly) that it was the central marker used by mapmakers to measure distances from Boston once it was installed here in 1737. In truth, the original milestone was set at the Old State House and modern mapmakers zero in on the center of the dome on the current State House. Just across Marshall Street at number 10 is the circa-1692 ***Ebenezer Hancock House,*** the oldest brick house in Boston, once owned by John Hancock. The ***Green Dragon Tavern*** at 11 Marshall Street is a long-removed descendent of an establishment by the same name where the Sons of Liberty and other rabble-rousers were wont to down a pint or two. Call (800) 543–9002.

On the southwest boundary of the Blackstone Block, where Union Street parallels Congress Street, the ***Union Oyster House*** building is rich with history. Built around 1714, it has been both domicile and business. From 1771 to 1775 the *Massachusetts Spy,* a newspaper of the Whig Party, was printed on the second floor. In 1798 the ground level was a tailor's shop; the Duke of Chartres lived upstairs, where he taught Boston merchants to speak French. He later returned to Paris via London and assumed the French throne as Louis Philippe. The nearby ***Bell-in-Hand Tavern*** at 45 Union Street was established in 1795, making it the oldest tavern in the city—although this was not the original site. Its first proprietor, Jimmy Wilson, was a Boston town crier. Call (617) 227–2098.

One of the great surprises of the Blackstone Block is the seamless and unobtrusive way the luxurious ***Bostonian Hotel*** manages to fit in. Preservationists' highly vocal fears were stilled when this sensitive, low-rise development opened in 1982. A few lobby displays reveal the layers of history and geology beneath the hotel; rotating exhibits sometimes show some of the artifacts uncovered when the foundation was excavated.

Places to Stay from Beacon Hill to Faneuil Hall Marketplace

Beacon Hill Hotel & Bistro,
19 Charles Street;
(617) 723–7575
or (888) 959–BHHB;
fax (617) 723–7525;

www.beaconhillhotel.com. The small bistro at street level puts a French accent on American fresh-market cooking. The bistro is open for breakfast daily 8:00 to 10:00 A.M., for lunch (or Sunday brunch) 11:30 A.M. to 1:30 P.M., and for dinner 5:30 to 11:00 P.M. Bistro: Moderate. Contemporary Art Deco styling informs the thirteen small but cozy rooms on the upper levels

that make you feel privileged to perch on Beacon Hill. Hotel: Expensive.

Charles Street Inn,
94 Charles Street;
(617) 314–8900
or (877) 772–8900;
fax (617) 371–0009;
www.charlestreetinn.com. Offering the best of twenty-first-century technology and comfort with the finest nineteenth-century styling, Charles Street Inn's eight

AUTHORS' FAVORITES FROM BEACON HILL TO FANEUIL HALL MARKETPLACE

African Meeting House

Nichols House Museum

Antiquarian Books of Boston

Museum of the Ancient and
Honorable Artillery

Holocaust Memorial

rooms each have carved marble fireplaces. Moderate to expensive.

Harborside Inn,
185 State Street;
(617) 723–7500;
fax (617) 670–2010;
www.hagopianhotels.com.
This magnificent stone-block warehouse between Quincy Market and Long Wharf holds fifty-four small-but-comfortable guest rooms with exposed brick walls and wooden floors. Moderate.

Omni Parker House,
60 School Street;
(617) 227–8600
or (800) THE–OMNI;
fax (617) 742–5729;
www.omnihotels.com.
The grandmother of all Boston grand hotels, the Omni Parker House underwent extensive renovations in 1999 to 2000 to brighten and, in many cases, enlarge the rooms. Moderate to expensive.

Regal Bostonian Hotel,
Faneuil Hall Marketplace;
(617) 523–3600
or (800) 343–0922;
fax (617) 523–2454;
www.millennium-hotels.
com.
The mazelike structure of the Regal Bostonian pro-

vides both character and privacy to its 201 rooms. Expensive.

XV Beacon,
15 Beacon Street;
(617) 670–1500
or (877) 992–3220;
fax (617) 670–2525;
www.xvbeacon.com.
At the pinnacle of Beacon Hill, XV Beacon is top form for lovers of high technology and postmodern design. It's also handy to the offices of Boston's intellectual rights attorneys and venture capitalists. Expensive.

Places to Eat from Beacon Hill to Faneuil Hall Marketplace

Bay Tower,
60 State Street;
(617) 723–1666.
The main dining room emphasizes luxury dishes such as a lobster-and-foie-gras terrine followed by sea bass dressed with osetra caviar. But you can save a few dollars by ordering from the abridged but still ambi-

tious menu at the upstairs lounge, where the jaw-dropping view of Boston Harbor is actually better and there's live music. Dining room open Monday through Thursday 5:30 to 10:00 P.M., Friday, 5:30 to 11:00 P.M., Saturday 5:00 to 11:00 P.M. Lounge open Monday through Thursday 5:00 P.M. to midnight, Friday and Saturday 5:00 P.M. to 1:00 A.M. Closed Sunday. Expensive.

Black Rose,
160 State Street;
(617) 742–2286.
Boston's reputation as an Irish-American city rests, in part, on the Black Rose, where the Guinness is fresh, the *craic* is good, and the food is what you'd expect in a bar. Open for lunch and dinner Monday through Saturday 11:30 A.M. to 2:00 A.M., Sunday noon to 2:00 A.M. Inexpensive to moderate.

Brigham's,
50 Congress Street;
(617) 523–9372.
See page 11 for full description.

Cafe Vanille,
70 Charles Street;
(617) 523–9200.
Sinfully rich Parisian-style

pastries, loaded with butter-cream or chocolate ganache, are Vanille's specialty. At midday, they also make sandwiches on crusty bread and offer a selection of soups and quiches. Open daily 6:30 A.M. to 7:00 P.M. Inexpensive.

Durgin-Park Restaurant,
South Market of Faneuil Hall Marketplace;
(617) 227–2038.
See page 12 for full description.

Kingfish Hall,
South Market,
Faneuil Hall Marketplace;
(617) 523–8862.
Restaurateur Todd English conquered the kingdom of Poseidon with this 200-seat seafood restaurant that's finally brought some life to its corner of Faneuil Hall Marketplace. No reservations are taken, so the wait can stretch an hour or more unless you arrive early or late. Open for lunch and dinner daily 11:00 A.M. to 10:00 P.M. Moderate.

Lala Rokh,
97 Mount Vernon Street;
(617) 720–5511.
Before there was great French food or great North African food, there was Persian cuisine—the spice-laden mother of all fine Western dining. Discover

the past (and maybe the future) of gourmet dining at Lala Rokh. Open for lunch Monday through Friday noon to 3:00 P.M., dinner daily 5:30 to 10:00 P.M. Moderate to expensive.

Maison Robert,
45 School Street;
(617) 227–3370.
Classical French haute cuisine receives a modern touch in a formal dining room set for special occasions. For much lower prices on bistro dishes with flair, head downstairs to Ben's Cafe, which sets up outdoor tables by the statue of Ben Franklin in warm weather. Open Monday through Friday for lunch 11:30 A.M. to 2:30 P.M., dinner 5:30 to 9:30 P.M. Closed Sunday. Ben's Cafe: Moderate. Maison Robert: Expensive.

Milk Street Cafe,
50 Milk Street;
(617) 542–2433.
Sandwich shops come and sandwich shops go, but the best of all is this long-timer, a dairy kosher deli beloved by downtown merchants and Financial District hotshots alike. Open Monday through Friday 7:00 A.M. to 3:00 P.M. Closed Saturday and Sunday. Inexpensive.

No. 9 Park,
9 Park Street;
(617) 742–9991.
Star chef and co-owner Barbara Lynch interprets the classics of Mediterranean cooking with signature gusto and finesse. State House politicians haunt the bar, but the food is so good that you can ignore them. Open for lunch Monday through Friday 11:30 A.M. to 2:30 P.M., for dinner Monday through Saturday 5:30 to 10:00 P.M. Closed Sunday. Expensive.

Panificio,
144 Charles Street;
(617) 227–4340.
This bakery's rustic Italian breads are the basis for light meals offered all day. Weekend brunch specialties include frittatas, French toast, and other egg dishes. Open Monday through Friday 7:00 A.M. to 10:00 P.M., Saturday and Sunday 10:00 A.M. to 6:00 P.M. Inexpensive.

Paramount Deli Restaurant,
44 Charles Street;
(617) 720–1152.
Jay Leno used to hang out at the Paramount when he was a student at Emerson College. The joint's grown up since, but bistro-style entrees such as chicken

AUTHORS' FAVORITE PLACES TO EAT FROM BEACON HILL TO FANEUIL HALL MARKETPLACE

| No. 9 Park | Durgin-Park Restaurant |
| Torch | Milk Street Cafe |

with boursin topped by a lemon-and-white-wine sauce are still some of the cheapest on Beacon Hill. Open for breakfast and lunch Monday through Saturday 7:00 A.M. to 4:30 P.M., Sunday 8:00 A.M. to 4:30 P.M., for dinner daily 5:30 to 10:00 P.M. Inexpensive to moderate.

Quincy Market Food Court,

Faneuil Hall Marketplace; no phone.
Almost every form of fast food known to humankind is available here, and much of it is surprisingly good. Some of it (the chowders, salads with dressing on the side) is even healthy. Order what you want and eat at tables beneath the elegant rotunda. Open for breakfast, lunch, and dinner Monday through Saturday 6:30 A.M. to 9:00 P.M., Sunday 10:00 A.M. to 6:00 P.M. Inexpensive to moderate.

Rustic Kitchen,

200 Quincy Market; (617) 523–6334.
In warm weather most diners opt for the outdoor cafe tables, but it's much more interesting to sit inside where you can watch chefs pulling dishes in and out of the wood-burning oven that is the centerpiece of both the room and the menu. Pizzas and pastas are supplemented with imaginative fish preparations, such as grouper crusted with an olive mixture and served with eggplant caponata. Open for lunch Monday through Friday 11:00 A.M. to 4:00 P.M., for brunch Sunday 11:00 A.M. to 3:00 P.M., for dinner Sunday 3:00 to 10:00 P.M., Monday through Thursday 4:00 to 10:00 P.M., and Friday and Saturday 4:00 to 11:00 P.M. Moderate.

The Sevens,

77 Charles Street; (617) 523–9074.
The Sevens is everything that the bar in Cheers! tried to be. It's Beacon Hill's true neighborhood pub, where there's an elbow-worn bar, nonstop television, and pewlike wooden booths where you can make a meal of deli sandwiches and a few pints. Open Monday through Saturday 11:30 A.M. to 1:00 A.M., Sunday noon to 1:00 A.M. Inexpensive.

75 Chestnut,

75 Chestnut Street; (617) 227–2175.
You can imagine you're in a Beacon Hill private dining room when you settle in at 75 Chestnut for a hearty herb-crusted rack of lamb or a wide bowl of pan-roasted scallops and mussels in chardonnay cream sauce. Open for dinner daily 5:30 to 10:00 P.M.; Sunday brunch is served from noon to 3:00 P.M. from September to June. Moderate to expensive.

Torch,

26 Charles Street; (617) 723–5939.
Chef/owner Evan Deluty cut his culinary teeth working in bistros in Paris, and he brings the look, taste, and feel to Beacon Hill. Open for dinner Tuesday through Thursday and Sunday 5:00 to 10:00 P.M., Friday and Saturday 5:00 to 10:30 P.M. Expensive.

Union Oyster House,

41 Union Street; (617) 227–2750.
See page 12 for full description.

Chinatown and the Financial District

Chinatown and the Financial District stand cheek-by-jowl south of Downtown Crossing and on the erstwhile mudflats that Boston's first settlers called South Cove. The juxtaposition between the intensely residential and commercial ethnic neighborhood and the glass canyons of high finance has a poetic symmetry, for the roots of much of Boston's early wealth lie in the city's trade with east Asia in the late eighteenth and early nineteenth centuries.

Both neighborhoods are comparatively young. Although Chinatown was recognizably Chinese as early as the 1880s, anti-immigration laws kept it from growing significantly until after World War II. Likewise, the Financial District burgeoned between the world wars, when the city eliminated some of the small streets in this former manufacturing district to consolidate lots large enough for skyscrapers.

Casual visitors rarely see either Chinatown or the Financial District. Both places have a secret life of their own, very different from nearby tourist districts, and both offer some wonderful dining opportunities. In fact, Chinatown is the city's premier neighborhood for late-night dining, and the Financial District has some of the best lunch spots and a handful of destination restaurants where the city's high rollers clinch their

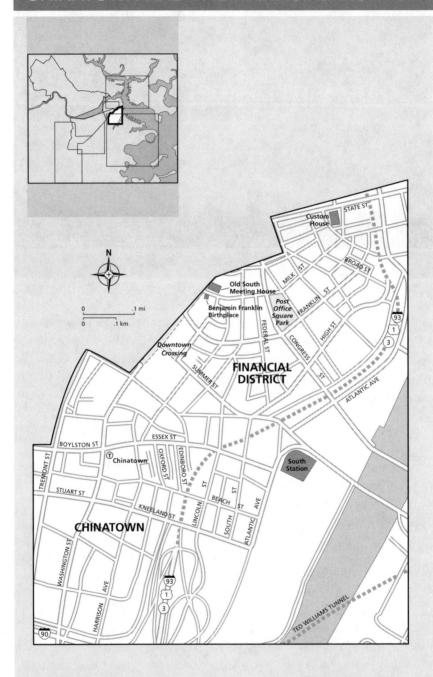

deals. Visit Chinatown anytime—the streets are almost always bustling. But save your trip to the Financial District for the nine-to-five weekday work day, when you can see the machinations of Boston's money managers.

Chinatown

Today's Chinatown is concentrated between Washington Street and the Surface Artery and between Essex and Kneeland Streets, although portions of the residential neighborhood persist west of Kneeland in the shadows of Tufts Medical Center. These boundaries will shift once the Big Dig is completed; Chinatown has already colonized the Leather District on the South Station side of the Surface Artery, and the prospect of a park at the site of the current turnpike ramp offers hope for new community open space in the most crowded neighborhood in Boston.

Immigrants to Chinatown tend to move out to the suburbs within a few generations, making way for the next wave of newcomers. Of the approximately 4,300 residents of Chinatown, 90 percent are ethnic Chinese, and of that group, three-quarters are immigrants from Hong Kong, Taiwan, or the People's Republic of China. The other 10 percent of the population has come mostly from Laos, Vietnam, Cambodia, Thailand, and other countries of southeast Asia, resulting in a proliferation of southeast Asian shops and restaurants among the older Chinese establishments.

The easiest place to begin a tour is at the Chinatown MBTA stop on the Orange Line at the corner of Essex and Washington streets (where Boylston Street changes name to Essex Street). Do as the Chinese do, and overlook the last vestiges of Boston's "combat zone" of show bars, peep shows, and adult magazine/video shops.

You'll want to stop first at the ***China Trade Center*** at 2 Boylston Street, opposite Washington Street from the Registry of Motor Vehicles. Here you

Where the Tree Stood Tall

A painted relief sculpture on the third level of the Registry of Motor Vehicles building on the corner of Washington and Essex Streets marks the spot where the **Liberty Tree** once stood. The Sons of Liberty used to gather beneath the massive oak or elm (sources disagree). In 1773 they assembled here in Indian garb and rowed from the shore 1 block away to launch the Boston Tea Party. Not surprisingly, the occupying British army cut the tree down in 1775.

head of the class

When the **Quincy School** at 90 Tyler Street opened in 1847, it was the first school in America where teachers had their own classrooms and students had their own desks instead of sitting together on benches.

can pick up a Chinatown map and business directory at the Chinatown Main Street office on the lower level. On the street level, take a look at the Chinese zodiac rendered in floor murals. The trade center hasn't really caught on in Chinatown, where life is lived out on the streets instead of inside minimalls. Take a leaf from the residents' book and plunge into the neighborhood.

One of the more atmospheric streets where commerce and residence converge is Oxford Street, which you'll reach by walking down Essex. About two-thirds of the way down Oxford Street, a small courtyard opens on the right to **Oxford Place,** where you'll find one of Chinatown's many striking murals. The wall-size painting, sponsored by the Chinese Economic Development Council, is based on a classic Chinese painting in the collection of Boston's Museum of Fine Arts, *Travellers in an Autumn Landscape* by Wang Yun (1652–1735). The private alleyway behind the courtyard harks back to the early days of Chinatown and its dense urban housing.

At 18–20 Oxford the **Sun Sun Co.** market (they'll scoop up fresh fish from the tank for you) occupies a landmark building that encapsulates Chinatown history in its successive uses. Originally a garment factory, it served from 1931 to 1984 as a school founded by Chinese businessmen to preserve the Chinese language and cultural traditions. The school has since relocated to the Quincy School site at 90 Tyler Street.

The next street that leads off Essex is **Ping On,** the "Alley of Peace and Security," where the Chinese workers who began arriving in 1875 pitched their tents. Shoe factory owners in Lawrence had brought them into the region to

Har-dee, har! har!

Self-proclaimed as America's oldest active joke shop, **Jack's Joke Shop** has been doing business since 1922, although many of its gags are much hoarier. Patronized by twelve-year-old boys of all ages, Jack's is the primo source for vampire teeth, Vulcan ears, snap-on snouts, the Bloody Blade (it drips blood inside a layer of clear vinyl), and all forms, shapes, and sizes of excrement (with or without flies). Jack's vies to keep au courant with fake lottery scratch tickets and a squirting computer mouse. Open Monday through Saturday 9:00 A.M. to 5:30 P.M., Jack's is at 226 Tremont Street; (617) 426–9640.

break a strike, then abandoned the men when the labor dispute was settled. Many Chinese gravitated to Boston and eventually found work laying America's first telephone cables. (Alexander Graham Bell invented the telephone nearby in the Financial District and established his first Bell Telephone offices at the edge of Chinatown.) A communal oven for roasting pigs stood on Ping On until the 1950s.

gettingsettled

The settlement house that stood at 93 Tyler Street, **Denison House,** was launched in 1892 to help immigrants earn a living by selling their crafts. When Amelia Earhart was a social worker at Denison House, she flew over Boston and showered the city with leaflets announcing a Denison House street fair.

When you turn right onto Edinboro Street, you'll immediately encounter **Oriental Arts & Crafts** at number 11 (617–728–8588). Chent Chow sells and frames traditional Chinese watercolors and brush-and-ink paintings here. Moreover, he also carves "chops"—the lovely stone stamps of the owner's signature. If your name is not Chinese, he will translate it into Chinese characters. His sets of stone and ink start around $50, including the carving.

Edinboro concludes at **Beach Street,** so-named because it was, indeed, the original shoreline in this part of Boston before South Cove was filled in during the nineteenth century. An ornate **Chinese Dragon Gate,** presented to Boston in 1982 by the Nationalist government of China based in Taiwan, marks

Dragon Gate

the entrance to Chinatown at the foot of Beach Street. Open telephone booths with a similar pagoda motif are located beneath the gate. You'll see these booths throughout Chinatown—remnants of an era before cell phones. The small park and playground just inside the gate is one of the few quiet gathering spots in bustling Chinatown. A 1970 mural behind a screen of hardy locust trees shows a sampan sailing against the wind.

Beach Street is Chinatown as most outsiders imagine it—a phantasmagoric succession of small shops with roast ducks hanging in the windows, herbalists behind their counters with glass jars of dried potions, fortune-tellers, bakeries, and fast-food shops.

As you walk up Beach Street, make a short detour onto Tyler Street. The ***Chinese Arts & Crafts Manufactory Outlet*** at 5 Tyler occupies the first building constructed exclusively for the Chinese community rather than converted from a previous use. The shop stocks an extensive selection of kung fu movies and Japanese animation in the video CD format that swept through Asia but never caught on in the United States.

Beach Street is a good place to seek out a casual lunch while puttering around the neighborhood. Our first choice is usually the tiny ***Rainbow Restaurant*** at 60 Beach Street (617–542–1763). The few Formica tables fill up quickly because the plates of rice and spare ribs (or roasted poultry) are excellent bargains. You can also pick up a whole roast duck or rack of pork spare ribs to take home. It's open Monday through Friday and Sunday 11:00 A.M. to 11:00 P.M.; Saturday 11:00 A.M. to 2:00 A.M.

Half of Chinatown seems to stop for lunch at the ***Chinatown Eatery,*** which is located in the physical and psychological heart of the neighborhood on the corner of Beach Street and Harrison Avenue (44–46 Beach Street).

Chinatown's Local Flavor

If you've ever wondered what to do with bitter melon, lotus root, lychee nuts, or other exotic produce that spills from the bins in Asian markets, sign up for a tour of Chinatown with Bik Ng and **Mein Dish Tours.** Born in southern China and raised in Hong Kong, Ng was taught to cook by her mother and grandmother and now shares her knowledge of traditional Chinese cuisine in the classes she teaches at the Cambridge School of Culinary Arts. Ng also leads small groups on tours of Chinatown, stopping in at markets, herbalists, bakeries, barbecue shops, and gift shops where visitors get a warm welcome from community members. The two-and-a-half-hour tours end with a dim sum feast. Tours are offered on Saturday and Sunday at 10:30 A.M. The $35 fee includes dim sum lunch. Visit www.meindish.com or send an e-mail to meindish@aol.com.

The dumpling sellers and other fast-food vendors here would probably operate from street carts in most cities—but there's no room on the street in Boston's Chinatown. The real standout is the *Juice Bar* on the second level. This countertop operation specializes in shakes and juices of Hong Kong and Hanoi—tasty treats such as a lychee freeze, adzuki (red bean) with milk, and mango juice. Open daily 9:00 A.M. to 11:00 P.M.

writing on the wall

The faces of Chinatown's past and present peer out from the **Community Unity mural** on the corner of Oak Street and Harrison Avenue behind a parking lot. It tells the history of the community, from women stitching clothing in the garment district to contract workers for the telephone company to scenes of contemporary life in Chinatown.

Nam Buk Hong Inc. at 75 Harrison Avenue (617–426–8227) is not the only Chinese herbal remedy shop in Chinatown, but it's the most prominent—sort of the Rexall of cure-alls. If you continue up Beach Street between Harrison Avenue and Washington Street, you'll also find a line of small, inexpensive restaurants serving Vietnamese soups. What the herbs won't cure, a steaming bowl of *pho* with lots of chopped basil and a pinch of hot pepper will.

Facing the end of Beach across Washington is another shop dedicated to your health. *Vinh Kan Ginseng Co.* at 675 Washington Street (617–338–9028) carries a remarkable variety of ginseng products—both American and Asian ginseng—as well as one of the best selections of Chinese black and green teas in Chinatown. Open Monday through Saturday 10:00 A.M. to 6:00 P.M., Sunday 11:00 A.M. to 5:00 P.M.

Kneeland Street (which changes its name to Stuart Street on the other side of Washington) is the main driving thoroughfare through Chinatown, linking Boston's theater district along Tremont Street to the Leather District on the south side of the Surface Artery. Kneeland is also one of Chinatown's primary commercial streets.

The stylish women of Chinatown head to *Kim's Fashion Design* at 12 Kneeland Street (617–426–5740) for their special-occasion wear. They can select from racks of ready-made dresses and jackets or opt to have an outfit custom-designed and tailored by the proprietress, who has her studio in the back. The shop specialty is embroidered silks. Open Monday to Friday 10:00 A.M. to 7:00 P.M., Saturday 11:00 A.M. to 6:00 P.M., Sunday 11:00 A.M. to 5:00 P.M.

If you hanker to know what drives teens into a dance frenzy in Hong Kong, then stop into *Star Music* at 26 Kneeland Street (617–338–1122). The CD selection includes all the latest heartthrob ballads and disco pop raging in Hong Kong and Taiwan, as well as the hit tunes of Seoul and Tokyo. But it's

Cutting Comedy

The old playhouses of Boston's Theater District on Tremont and Boylston Streets at the edge of Chinatown represent the most architecturally eminent group of early theaters in America. They're usually lit with touring shows or Broadway tryouts. The all-time record-breaking run is **Shear Madness,** a comedy "whodunit" set in a hair salon. This show has played at the Charles Playhouse since the early 1980s. Show times are Sunday at 3:00 and 7:30 P.M., Tuesday through Friday at 8:00 P.M., Saturday at 6:30 and 9:30 P.M. The Charles is at 74 Warrenton Street. Call (617) 426–5225; www.shearmadness.com.

hard to say which is more popular here with Chinatown teens—the Asian pop or the two booths that make sheets of photo stickers. Open Monday through Saturday 10:00 A.M. to 7:00 P.M., Sunday 11:00 A.M. to 5:00 P.M.

On the other hand, if your idea of movement is more disciplined than the dance floor, head a few doors down. **Silky Way** at 38 Kneeland Street (617–423–2264) caters to martial arts enthusiasts with robes and garb, martial arts gear, instructional videos, and magazines. Silky Way can also help you find an instructor. Open Monday through Friday 9:00 A.M. to 6:00 P.M., Saturday 10:00 A.M. to 6:00 P.M., closed Sunday.

Farther down the street, heading toward the Leather District, **Jit An Tong Chinese Herbs** at 66 Kneeland Street (617–451–5228) stands out among the high-tech phone stores and electronics shops. With an apothecary counter on the right and a stairway on the left, this survivor of old Chinatown has a state-licensed acupuncturist practicing on the second floor. Call for an appointment.

Midnight Meat Loaf

A surprising number of Chinatown restaurants keep serving until 2:00 or even 3:00 A.M., but if you have a post-midnight hankering for food that you can't eat with chopsticks, cross the Surface Artery to visit **South Street Diner** at 178 Kneeland Street (617–350–0038). A real diner, right down to the quilted metal walls, greasy griddle, and line of stools at a long counter, South Street is open around the clock and serves breakfast at all hours—along with other foods properly washed down with a big mug of coffee. The night-owl crowd includes many Leather District coders (for those not in the know, a "coder" is someone who writes digital—i.e., computer—code) who are, in fact, on their coffee breaks. Coders and late-night cab drivers alike gravitate to the "Firebird" jukebox that sits in front of a cardboard likeness of James Dean and features sing-along favorites from the 1950s forward. Inexpensive.

You'll have to cross the Surface Artery to reach the Leather District. The patch of Lincoln, Utica, and South Streets where Boston's shoemaking industry once flourished is an area in transition. The warehouse and factory lofts of its spacious buildings have long attracted artists and for the last decade have enticed internet start-ups as well. As the lines blur between art and computer code, it can be hard to tell the artists from the coders in the Leather District. As a general rule, the commercial techies are the ones who can afford to rent the beautiful overhead loft spaces and then turn to places like *JMW Gallery* at 144 Lincoln Street (617–338–9097) to furnish them. JMW specializes in Arts and Crafts period furniture and ceramics. It's one of the few places where you can discover Grueby or Chelsea Tile Company ceramics—Arts and Crafts masters from the Boston area. Open Tuesday through Friday 11:00 A.M. to 6:00 P.M., Saturday 11:00 A.M. to 5:00 P.M.

Perhaps the signature space of the Leather District is **Les Zygomates Wine Bar & Bistro** at 129 South Street (617–542–5108). Named for the facial muscles that you use to smile, Les Zyg settled here before the Leather District had cachet. It helped make the neighborhood a destination for lovers of good wine and French bistro cuisine—not to mention the live jazz six nights a week. Open Monday through Friday 11:30 A.M. to 1:00 A.M., Saturday 6:00 P.M. to 1:00 A.M., closed Sunday. Moderate to Expensive.

Financial District

Boston's first financial district ran the length of State Street. At the head of the street stood the Old State House, where financiers met in the basement and waited for their ships to come into Long Wharf at the foot of the street. In between, the government took its cut at the Custom House. As Boston wealth grew, banks sprang up along State Street and other financial management companies spread into the adjoining streets. But the Great Fire of 1872 consumed sixty-five acres of old Boston and turned most of the district to cinders. The fire began on Summer Street and destroyed most of Franklin, Congress, and Federal streets. Physician and literary commentator Oliver Wendell Holmes bore witness in horror. "I saw the fire eating its way straight toward my deposits," he wrote. As a result, most of the Financial District we see today postdates that conflagration. The skyscraper park around Post Office

firstmoneydown

Boston's first bank, the Massachusetts Bank, opened in 1784. It is one of the ancestors of Bank of America.

Square is the product of economic booms in the 1920s and 1980s, when Boston's deep pockets reached for the sky.

The perfect gateway to the Financial District is **South Station,** the combined Amtrak passenger train and MBTA Red Line subway station. The great curving mass of the station embodied the heady romance of train travel when the building was erected in 1899. With the late-twentieth-century decline in rail service, South Station fell into tired decrepitude before a 1989 restoration gave it new life. The shops and interior food court have combined with revived interest in rail travel to make the station's soaring lobby one of the most dynamic places in town.

onguard

The Federal Reserve Bank of Boston has a security force equal to that of a small town.

Across Summer Street from South Station rises the great glass-and-aluminum shaft of the **Federal Reserve Bank of Boston** at 600 Atlantic Avenue. Look closely at this pedestrian-friendly skyscraper. The projecting aluminum spandrels of the tower serve as sunshades for the rooms inside, but they also help ameliorate the stiff downdraft that is characteristic of such buildings, thereby dramatically reducing ground-level winds.

One of twelve regional banks in the Federal Reserve system, this central bank for New England processes $65 billion in cash, checks, and electronic transfers every day, using specialized machinery that scrutinizes every single piece of currency

earlycall

In 1878 the Boston Stock Exchange first listed AT&T, just two years after Alexander Graham Bell invented the telephone.

that comes through the building to determine if it's fit to continue in circulation. If not (and a third of the one-dollar bills aren't), the serial number is recorded and the bill is whisked away to be shredded. The machines also catch about fifty counterfeit bills each day. Tours of the Federal Reserve were discontinued due to security concerns. Call (617) 973–3464 to see if they have been reinstated.

Cross Atlantic Avenue and proceed to the corner of Federal and High Streets for a reminder of Boston's past eminence as a manufacturing center. This trapezoidal Art Deco skyscraper was the first building to benefit from Boston's revision to its height restriction laws in 1928. (The new laws permitted taller buildings if they were set back from the street.) But the best part is at street

Financial District, South Station

level, where the **United Shoe Machinery** building is emblazoned with heroic bronze bas-reliefs of mythical figures and shoemaking machinery.

If you follow Summer Street to Devonshire, this canyon will bring you to the **Boston Stock Exchange,** which has an entrance at 201 Devonshire Street. Traders place and fill orders for 2,000 nationally listed equities and 200 high-growth companies at this third-oldest stock exchange in the United States. Working quietly at computer terminals, brokers buy and sell more than twenty million shares of stock daily. The Visitors' Gallery has been closed due to security concerns. Call (617) 235–2000 to see if it has been reopened.

Across Franklin Street, the **State Street Trust** building at 75 Federal Street was finished just before the 1929 Wall Street crash that ushered in the Great Depression. Conceived in more flush times, this epitome of Art Deco has been dwarfed by a massive addition but retains its posh lobby of golden- and black-colored marble with classic Deco signage.

It's hard to miss the looming building and black-granite bank at the corner of Franklin and Congress Streets, where a welcoming plaza (where financial workers sit to eat their lunches) compensates for the sheer bulk of the structure. The preamble to the U.S. Constitution is etched in 4-inch-high letters in the pavers in front of a fountain as a tribute to the Lane Street Meeting House that once stood here. In 1788 the Massachusetts delegates to the Constitutional Convention met there to ratify the document.

money in the bank

Boston is the country's second largest center for investment management, thanks to the presence of such firms as Fidelity, John Hancock, Liberty, Moors & Cabot, Putnam, Scudder, and State Street.

A lot of history surrounds the triangular green of **Post Office Square.** This stretch of grass is perhaps the most successful newer green space in central Boston and a favorite warm-weather lunch spot for financial workers. Across Congress Street from FleetBoston, the **Verizon building** at 185 Franklin Street is a handsome Art Moderne structure from 1947. Its historic treasures, however, are inside. Look up as you enter the oval lobby, surrounded by Dean Cornwall's 1951 mural *Telephone Men and Women at Work,* a 160-foot painted frieze of life-size figures. Off the lobby near the entrance, the company has preserved **Alexander Graham Bell's original laboratory,** which was relocated here when Bell's building on nearby Court Street was demolished. It's decidedly low-tech, but nonetheless amazing. Bell's presence is so palpable that he seems to have just stepped out the door, and visitors feel as if they have been transported back to 1876, when the inventor was applying for his first telephone patent (also displayed). Among the devices under glass is the machine on which Bell made the first call on March 10, 1876, telling his assistant, "Come here, Watson, I want you!" The building is open around the clock.

Post Office Square is flanked by two other magnificent buildings—the Art Deco **post office** building with its majestic geometric and botanical ornamentation and the former Federal Reserve Bank, a Renaissance Revival block now housing the **Langham Hotel.** The interior of the Langham preserves such original features as the painted dome and gold-leaf vaults of the foyer, N. C. Wyeth murals, and marble door frames and mantelpieces—seamlessly transforming a temple of money into a temple for the moneyed.

If you stroll up the edge of Post Office Square to its triangular tip, you can cut down Water Street to the **Custom House.** The base of the building dates

Mutual Benefit

The first pooled investment fund in the United States was formed in 1893 to benefit the faculty and staff of Harvard University, but the modern mutual fund wasn't invented until 1924, when three stock salesmen created Massachusetts Investors Trust. When the MIT made its debut in March of that year, it had $50,000 in assets and owned forty-five stocks. The major innovation of the mutual fund was to democratize investing by pooling investors' money to purchase stocks and then allowing investors to redeem fund shares at rates based on the underlying value of the stocks. The Depression slowed the initial growth of mutual funds, but the Fidelity Fund nonetheless was introduced in 1930. It eventually expanded to become **Fidelity Investments,** with corporate offices at 82 Devonshire Street. As of early 2001, Fidelity managed more than a trillion dollars in assets.

from 1835; the 1915 tower was Boston's first "skyscraper." Now a Marriott-managed condominium hotel, the Custom House has a small display of art and artifacts from Salem's Peabody Essex Museum, including maritime paintings, Chinese vases, and navigational instruments. At 10:00 A.M. and 4:00 P.M. Sunday through Friday and 4:00 P.M. on Saturday, you can also take a tour of the tower, which offers a 360-degree panorama of Boston. The $1.00 "donation" goes to charity. The Custom House has turned out to be the most productive *nesting site* in the eastern United States *for the endangered peregrine falcon.* Recognizing how the tower resembled the bird's cliffside habitat, wildlife biologists placed a wooden, gravel-lined box on a twenty-sixth-floor ledge more than a decade ago. Scores of chicks have since hatched here, taking wing to colonize much of the Northeast. The resident falcons on Throgs Neck Bridge in New York and on a casino building in Atlantic City, New Jersey, were hatched and fledged at the Custom House—feathered reminders of the ripple effects of Boston's financial clout.

Places to Stay in Chinatown and the Financial District

Langham Hotel,
250 Franklin Street;
(617) 451–1900 or
(800) 543–4300;
www.langhamhotels.com/boston. With its posh comfort in the French style, the Langham maintains the grandeur of the original Federal Reserve Bank building. Because it is a business hotel first and foremost, reduced rates are often available on weekends. Expensive.

Swissôtel Boston,
One Avenue de Lafayette;
(617) 451–2600 or
(800) 621–9200;
www.swissotel.com.
Built like a fortress, the Swissôtel is most easily entered from its parking garage, not from the street. But it is a true luxury hotel well located just a few minutes' walk to Chinatown, the Theater District, and the shopping area of Downtown Crossing. Security-minded business travelers like the key-access upper floors with their sweeping views. Expensive.

Tremont Boston Wyndham Hotel,
275 Tremont Street;
(617) 426–1400 or
(877) 999-3223;
www.wyndham.com.
With 322 rooms, this imposing 1925 hotel across from the Wang Center often caters to large bus groups. The refurbished lobby is grand, the rooms more simple. Moderate to expensive.

Wyndham Boston,
89 Broad Street;
(617) 556–0006 or
(800) 996–3246;
www.wyndham.com.
A former office building in the Financial District's signature Art Deco style, this is a top-of-the-line Wyndham, coupling many of the original details (marble floors, for example) with contemporary furnishings and baths. Moderate to expensive.

AUTHORS' FAVORITES IN CHINATOWN AND THE FINANCIAL DISTRICT

Post Office Square Park	Verizon mural and telephone museum
Mei Tung Oriental Food Super Market	Boston Stock Exchange
Custom House Tower	Federal Reserve Bank tour

Places to Eat in Chinatown and the Financial District

Bakey's,

45 Broad Street;
(617) 426–1710.
Something of a Financial District institution, Bakey's is a cozy, old-fashioned lunchroom by day (soup and sandwiches, mostly) and a friendly neighborhood bar with good pub food at night. Open Monday through Friday 11:30 A.M. to 7:00 P.M., closed Saturday and Sunday. Inexpensive.

Chau Chow City Restaurant,

83 Essex Street;
(617) 338–8158.
It's amazing how many people can pack into this space. The upper level ranks among Boston's best dim sum palaces (with perfect shrimp dumplings), while the lower levels serve contemporary Hong Kong seafood dishes, such as scallops with green beans and macadamia nuts. Open Sunday through Thursday

8:30 A.M. to 3:00 A.M., Friday and Saturday 8:30 A.M. to 4:00 A.M. Moderate.

Chinatown Eatery,

44–46 Beach Street; no phone. See page 22 for full description.

Cindy's Planet,

70 Tyler Street;
(617) 338–8837.
Ostensibly a sandwich shop, Cindy's is tops in Chinatown for "pearl drinks"—those trendy flavored shakes with bits of gelatinous pearl tapioca lurking at the bottom. They come in many fruit and nut flavors as well as Ovaltine and Horlick's. Open Tuesday through Friday 8:30 A.M. to 6:00 P.M., Saturday 11:00 A.M. to 6:00 P.M., Sunday 10:00 A.M. to 6:00 P.M., Monday 8:30 A.M. to 3:00 P.M. Inexpensive.

Cosí,

133 Federal Street;
(617) 292–2674.
This New York–based chain of sandwich shops raises the ante for delectable fast food for lunch. They fill their freshly baked Italian flat breads to order with tasty vegetables, meats, and cheeses. This Financial District branch has great

outdoor patio seating by a fountain and sometimes even serenades diners with a small jazz combo. Open Monday through Friday 7:00 A.M. to 5:00 P.M., closed Saturday and Sunday. Inexpensive.

Eldo Cake House,

36 Harrison Avenue;
(617) 350–7977.
Here's a bakery where you can get a whole meal by starting with the roast-pork or shredded-beef steamed buns and enjoying some lotus seed paste turnovers for dessert. The house specialties, though, are the airy cakes filled with whipped cream or chestnut cream. Open Monday through Saturday 7:00 A.M. to 6:30 P.M., Sunday 8:00 A.M. to 6:30 P.M. Inexpensive.

Hu Tien Nam-Vang,

7 Beach Street;
(617) 422–0501.
The beef-and-tendon soup with basil and sprouts on the side (a version of pho) will easily feed two people, and the rice and noodle plates are a similarly good deal. The only question is whether you can get a seat at this popular Vietnamese restaurant, especially at lunchtime. Open Sunday

through Thursday 8:30 A.M.
to 10:00 P.M., Friday and
Saturday 8:00 A.M. to 10:30
P.M. Inexpensive.

International Place Food Court,

Oliver and High Streets;
no phone.
When the weather outside
makes a picnic seem less
than attractive, this office-
building-atrium food court,
with tables grouped around
an indoor waterfall, is a
delightful and inexpensive
place to have lunch. Open
Monday through Friday
7:00 A.M. to 4:00 P.M.,
closed Saturday and
Sunday. Inexpensive.

King Fung Garden,

74 Kneeland Street;
(617) 357–5262.
This tiny room with red vinyl
seats may look very mod-
est, but their Mongolian hot
pots are a major hit, especially in cold weather. Open
daily 11:00 A.M. to
10:00 P.M. Inexpensive.

Les Zygomates Wine Bar & Bistro,

129 South Street;
(617) 542–5108.
See page 25 for full
description.

Milk Street Cafe,

Post Office Square Park;
(617) 350–7275.
This dairy kosher sandwich
shop is beloved in Boston
for its egg-salad and tuna-
salad sandwiches. The location can't be beat for a picnic lunch. Open Monday
through Friday 7:00 A.M. to
5:00 P.M., closed Saturday
and Sunday. Inexpensive.

New Shanghai Restaurant,

21 Hudson Street;
(617) 338–6688.
Ever wonder where Boston-
area superchefs go on their
night off? They're in New
Shanghai, feasting on Hong
Kong–trained chef C. K.
Sau's modern twists on traditional cooking, such as
baby eels in orange sauce.
The white linen tablecloths
signal that New Shanghai is
more formal than most
Chinatown restaurants.
Open daily 11:00 A.M. to
10:00 P.M. Moderate to
expensive.

News,

150 Kneeland Street;
(617) 426–6397.
This former diner has been
reimagined as a martini bar
with modernist sass and an
evening menu that runs
from decadent lobster to
sushi made on the spot.
During the daytime, News

caters to local office workers, so it's best to stick with
good sandwiches like the
super-thick turkey club,
designer salads (greens with
pine nuts and feta) in pre-
tilted bowls, or the always-
available breakfast menu.
One diner standard that's
carried over into the twenty-
first century is a truly great
chocolate cake. Open
Sunday through Thursday
11:00 A.M. to 4:00 A.M.,
continuously from Friday
11:00 A.M. to Sunday
5:00 A.M. Moderate.

Peach Farm Restaurant,

4 Tyler Street;
(617) 482–1116.
Cantonese delicacies that
are usually impossible to
find in suburban Chinese
restaurants bring Chinese
Americans swarming in to
eat at Peach Farm. Where
else are you going to get
sesame-tossed jellyfish
with sweet daikon pickles?
Open daily 11:00 A.M. to
3:00 A.M. Moderate.

Penang,

685 Washington Street;
(617) 451–6373.
One thing many immigrants
from southern Asia share is
a love for Malay cooking.
Penang scores with the theater going crowd, neighborhood residents, and young

AUTHORS' FAVORITE PLACES TO EAT IN CHINATOWN AND THE FINANCIAL DISTRICT

Bakey's	Rainbow Restaurant
King Fung	New Shanghai Restaurant
Les Zygomates	Radius

folks looking for a good-but-not-too-expensive date destination. The noodle dishes are a steal and the steamed fish is dreamy with spices. We're fond of the chicken in a hot, sweet, and sour mango sauce. Open Sunday through Thursday 10:30 A.M. to 11:30 P.M., Friday and Saturday 11:30 A.M. to midnight. Moderate.

Radius,
8 High Street;
(617) 426–1234.
Chef and co-owner Michael Schlow is usually one step ahead of upscale gastronomic trends, providing an insider's preview of the next taste sensations that will sweep the foodie community. The restaurant is decorated in roughly the same palette used for Rolls-Royce automobiles, making it seem no doubt homey for the bankers, traders, and venture capitalists who come here to seal their deals with caviar and champagne. Open for lunch Monday through Friday 11:30 A.M. to 2:30 P.M., for dinner Monday through Friday 5:30 to 10:00 P.M.,

Saturday 5:30 to 11:00 P.M. Expensive.

Rainbow Restaurant,
60 Beach Street;
(617) 542–1763.
See page 22 for full description.

Sakura-Bana Japanese Restaurant,
57 Broad Street;
(617) 542–4311.
Look for lines out the door at lunch as junior financiers queue up for take-out sushi. Evening fare leans toward tempura and rice and noodle plates. Open for lunch Monday through Friday 11:30 A.M. to 2:30 P.M., for dinner daily 5:00 to 10:00 P.M. Moderate.

South Street Diner,
178 Kneeland Street;
(617) 350–0038.
See page 24 for full description.

Sultan's Kitchen,
72 Broad Street;
(617) 728–2828.
Grilled lamb kebabs, baba ganoush, and rice-stuffed grape leaves in pita bread are the tip of the iceberg at one of Boston's few Turkish

restaurants. Lunch take-out lines are long, but stop by after the rush for stuffed baked eggplant, *patlican iman bayildi*. Open Monday through Friday 11:00 A.M. to 5:00 P.M., Saturday 11:00 A.M. to 3:00 P.M., closed Sunday. Inexpensive.

Vault Restaurant,
105 Water Street;
(617) 292–9966.
The name is a no-brainer—the restaurant is literally inside a former bank vault. The corkscrew sign out front is a tipoff to the room's wide-ranging and sensibly priced wine list. The menu is scrupulously seasonal—if it's not at the peak of ripeness, you can't order it—and the dishes draw heavily on classics of the Tuscan table like spaghettini tossed with codfish and sprinkled with chile flakes and garlic. Open for lunch Monday through Friday 11:30 A.M. to 2:30 P.M., for dinner Monday through Saturday 5:30 to 10:00 P.M., closed Sunday. Moderate to expensive.

Back Bay and Fenway

It's no coincidence that the subway and streetcar routes serving the Back Bay and the Fenway are variants of the MBTA's Green Line, for these are among Boston's greenest neighborhoods. After more than two centuries huddled on the nubby hills of the Shawmut peninsula, the city created (through landfill) several square miles of new land in the nineteenth century and proceeded to "stretch out." For the first time in Boston's history, neighborhoods were created with a master plan, imparting a sense of order and decorum here that the rest of the city defies.

Even though they abut each other, Back Bay and the Fenway are surprisingly different. Back Bay possesses an organizational logic borrowed liberally from Paris—arrow-straight avenues punctuated at regular intervals by cross streets named in ascending alphabetical order. The Fenway, on the other hand, follows the fens of the Muddy River. Water winds and wends its way to sea, and so does the park around which the Fenway was built.

Back Bay

Back Bay is one of the most heavily visited areas in Boston—and no wonder. It possesses some of the city's finest architecture,

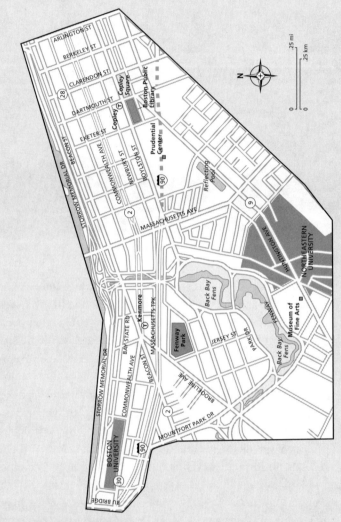

ARLINGTON ST
BERKELEY ST
CLARENDON ST
DARTMOUTH ST
EXETER ST
Copley
Copley Square
Boston Public Library
Prudential Center
Reflecting Pool
STORROW MEMORIAL DR
BEACON ST
COMMONWEALTH AVE
NEWBURY ST
BOYLSTON ST
MASSACHUSETTS AVE
Kenmore
MASSACHUSETTS TPK
BAY STATE RD
BEACON ST
Fenway Park
JERSEY ST
PARK DR
Back Bay Fens
Back Bay Fens
Museum of Fine Arts
HUNTINGTON AVE
NORTHEASTERN UNIVERSITY
FENWAY
BROOKLINE AVE
COMMONWEALTH AVE
STORROW MEMORIAL DR
BOSTON UNIVERSITY
BU BRIDGE
MOUNTFORT PARK DR

.25 mi
.25 km

N

two major retail streets, a convention center, and a cluster of superb hotels. Moreover, the long green strip of the Commonwealth Avenue mall cuts through the entire neighborhood, from the Public Garden to Massachusetts

artfully seated

Isabella Stewart Gardner and her husband always sat in seats A-15 and A-16 in the balcony of Symphony Hall.

Avenue, while Copley Square provides Boston's finest ceremonial plaza. When thousands of Boston Marathon runners set out each April from Hopkinton, they plan to run all the way to Copley Square.

We suggest that you do the same—or, better yet, hop on the Green Line and ride to the Copley/BPL stop. Back Bay presents Boston's most architecturally distinct face to the world, but you can go behind the facades to some of the lesser-known corners of one of the city's best-known neighborhoods. The heart of it all is Copley Square, named for painter John Singleton Copley, who was born near here in 1737. (We say "near" because the present site of the square was under water at high tide in Copley's day.)

Two buildings define Copley Square, facing off over the plaza like protagonists in a freshman essay comparing and contrasting humanism and religious faith: the Boston Public Library and Trinity Church. Admittedly, neither is off the beaten path, yet portions of each building are less well trod than others.

The first significant free municipal library in the United States, the **Boston Public Library (BPL)** moved into its Copley Square digs in 1895. The building was commissioned at $400,000 but cost $2.5 million by the time it was done. The city intended it as a palace of the people, and that's what architect Richard McKim gave them. More than a century later, it remains a marvel of the decorative arts. It's well worth taking a free "Art and Architecture" tour to see the striking allegorical murals by John Singer Sargent, Edward Abbey, and Puvis de Chavannes. The tours begin inside the

call them "sir"

Back Bay streets are named for English noblemen.

Dartmouth Street entrance on Copley Square on Monday at 2:30 P.M., Tuesday and Thursday at 6:00 P.M., and Friday and Saturday at 11:00 A.M. The tour is also offered from October through May on Sunday at 2:00 P.M. Call (617) 536–5400, extension 2216.

But there are treasures hidden in the library that tours often miss. If you're on your own, enter through the Dartmouth Street doors and climb the

heard on mass ave

Compositions given their world premieres by the Boston Symphony Orchestra at Symphony Hall on Massachusetts Avenue in the Fenway include Symphony No. 4, Opus 47 by Sergei Prokofiev (1930), Concerto for Orchestra by Bela Bartok (1944), Symphony No. 3 by Aaron Copland (1946), Symphony No. 2, The Age of Anxiety, by Leonard Bernstein (1949), and The Mask of Time by Sir Michael Tippett (1984).

magnificent staircase guarded by lions. On the second level is a small stairway that ascends to the third floor, where few visitors venture except to see the Sargent murals. Even most Bostonians don't realize that in addition to the 65 miles of shelved books, the city library has an outstanding collection of artwork. The **Wiggin Gallery** highlights selections from the collection of prints and drawings in rotating exhibitions. At the back of the gallery are small dioramas depicting printmakers at work. Among the subjects are James McNeill Whistler outside the gates of the Luxembourg Gardens, Henri de Toulouse-Lautrec making drawings of the circus, George Bellows watching a boxing match, and Honoré Daumier looking down on a Paris street from his window. The Wiggin Gallery is open during the BPL's usual hours: Monday through Thursday 9:00 A.M. to 9:00 P.M., Friday and Saturday 9:00 A.M. to 5:00 P.M., Sunday noon to 5:00 P.M. in the fall and winter. Call (617) 536–5400.

Follow the signs from the print gallery to the Rare Book Room, pausing to look down from the windows onto the library's central courtyard. You'll pass through the **Koussevitzky Room,** which displays musical scores, ballet and opera photographs, and other memorabilia of the man who conducted the Boston Symphony Orchestra from 1924 until 1949. One of the champions of

Bright Forecast

There's no missing the high-rise, glass-skinned "new" John Hancock tower across Stuart Street from Trinity Church, no matter how hard it tries to disappear. The older **John Hancock Tower** (built in 1947), a block away at 175 Berkeley Street, is also unmistakable, thanks to the weather beacon on its truncated pyramid top:

Steady blue, clear view.

Flashing blue, clouds are due.

Steady red, rain ahead.

Flashing red, snow instead.

(During the summer, flashing red means that the Red Sox game has been canceled.)

twentieth-century orchestral music, Koussevitzky commissioned major works from Aaron Copland, a young Leonard Bernstein, and his longtime friends Igor Stravinsky and Joseph-Maurice Ravel. Koussevitzky's reconstructed office is visible behind glass.

There's something magical about the **Rare Book Room,** rather like entering the inner sanctum of a bibliophile's dream world. President John Adams's library surrounds the room on a mezzanine, and the holdings include a first edition of Charles Darwin's *The Origin of Species* that was "borrowed" in the 1920s and returned to the library in 2001. (The overdue fines were waived. . . .) You'll need a reason, a photo ID, and a BPL borrower's card to look over items from the collection, which includes more than a hundred of comedian Jack Benny's droll letters that inevitably leave readers trying to stifle their involuntary chortles. Even if you're not on a research mission, stop in to examine the rotating thematic exhibitions that highlight aspects of the collection. The Rare Book Room is open Monday through Friday 9:00 A.M. to 5:00 P.M., closed Saturday and Sunday.

The BPL's hidden inner courtyard has long been a favorite place for Bostonians to enjoy a serene brown-bag lunch while listening to the splash and burble of the central fountain. They might also contemplate the city's puritanical ways while gazing on the exuberant statue of Bacchante. Created by Frederick MacMonnies, the work was originally placed in the courtyard in 1896. But the nude—and seemingly intoxicated—figure was deemed inappropriate for a temple of learning and was donated to the Metropolitan Museum of Art in Manhattan. About a century after Bacchante's banishment, a replica was returned to the courtyard.

Perhaps another sign of the library's more relaxed ways is the opening of two dining areas in the gracious old rooms of the McKim building. If you were ever admonished not to eat or drink in the library, you will surely want to help yourself to a full buffet lunch in the Novel Restaurant or just take a break with coffee and dessert in the adjacent Map Room Café. **Novel Restaurant** is open Monday through Friday from 11:30 A.M. to 4:30 P.M. and the **Map Room Café** is open Monday through Saturday from 9:00 A.M. to 5:00 P.M. Call (617) 385– 5660. Inexpensive.

Across Copley Square, the granite-and-sandstone Romanesque edifice of **Trinity Church** was so immediately admired on its completion in 1877 that H. H. Richardson's neo-medieval design spawned two generations of similar churches around the country. Although dwarfed by nearby modern skyscrapers, Trinity maintains a squat dignity. Most visitors poke their heads in to see the fine stained-glass windows in the Arts and Crafts style by John LaFarge, among others, but they miss the hundreds of details that make the church such

weightofprayer

The tower of Trinity Church weighs 90 million pounds.

a landmark. If you pick up the self-guided-tour brochure ($3.00), you'll see it all. Even better, call ahead to see what time the daily guided tours are being offered. There is always a free tour on Sunday after the 11:15 A.M. service. Self-guided tours are permitted daily from 8:00 A.M. to 6:00 P.M. unless a service is in progress. Guided and self-guided tours are $4.00. Call (617) 536–0944. On Fridays from mid-September to mid-June, there's an organ concert at noon; donation requested.

Be sure to check out the ***Trinity Church bookstore*** for recordings of organ and choral concerts, Christmas ornaments showing architectural details, and silk scarves and notecards of the stunning windows. The store is open Monday through Saturday 9:00 A.M. to 6:00 P.M., Sunday 10:00 A.M. to 6:00 P.M.

Trinity Church

Before leaving Copley Square, you might want to stroll through the ***Fairmont Copley Plaza Hotel*** just to see the glittering 5,000-square-foot lobby with its 21-foot-high gilded ceiling. The fully restored hotel epitomizes Edwardian-era glamour and actually hosts more weddings every year than Trinity Church. If it's open, also have a look at the ***Oak Room*** restaurant, where generations of Boston families have marked special occasions by dining within this dark-paneled "inner sanctum" where mirrors reflect the sumptuous draperies and Waterford crystal chandeliers.

If you cross Clarendon Street behind Trinity Church and proceed to the corner of Boylston Street, you'll see ***the New England building*** at 501 Boylston Street, notable less for its facade than for the history lessons hidden in its lobby, which is open around the clock. Past the elevators, ***dioramas of local history*** depict Native Americans catching fish in a weir on this exact site between 2,000 and 3,600 years ago. The scene is based on archaeologists' conjectures, which in turn were based on the 65,000 sharpened wooden stakes found here during excavations for the subway system in 1913 and for the New England's foundation in 1939. Other dioramas show the filling in of Back Bay (1858), construction of the Boston Society of Natural History (now the clothier Louis) as land in the background is being filled in (1863), and the house of William Blaxton (1625), Boston's first settler. The outer lobby walls are covered with stirring 1943 murals, including *Paul Revere Gives the Alarm, Washington Takes Command in Cambridge,* and *Launching of the Frigate "Constitution."*

Another hidden delight lurks within the unlikely facade of the building on the corner of Berkeley and Boylston Streets, a few steps down Berkeley from the giant bronze teddy bear statue. The aptly named ***Winter Garden*** is actually the building's central atrium, with a Rebecca's Cafe and plenty of seating on the second level beneath the glass ceiling. The marble columns and floors give the space a light formality that makes a wonderful respite from winter weather or an escape from the crowds in any season.

For a look at one of the more amazing pieces of building decoration in Boston, walk down Berkeley Street and turn left on Stuart Street. The door to the ***Salada Tea building*** at 330 Stuart Street

Salada Tea Building

is covered with ornate bronze reliefs showing tea workers and elephants. The surrounding stonework contains more elephant motifs.

Back on Boylston Street, heading toward the Public Garden, the building with the fancifully painted facade at number 356 was long the home of the **Women's Educational & Industrial Union,** a survivor from Boston's Victorian-era social reform movement. It was established in 1877 by one of the country's first female physicians, Dr. Harriet Clisby, to head off the exploitation of women and children in an era of rapid industrialization and population growth. The organization opened its Shop at the Union that year so women could market foodstuffs and home crafts to support themselves and their children. Times have changed, and the handicrafts shop began to drain the organization's resources more than it contributed to the bottom line. In 2004 the organization put the building on the market to raise enough funds to move into more modern offices where it could establish a technology training center more in sync with the core mission of promoting economic self-sufficiency. At the time this book went to press, the Shop at the Union was set to close in the summer of 2004.

At the corner of Arlington and Boylston Streets, the **Arlington Street Church** is generally considered the "mother church" of Unitarianism in the United States. Inspired by St. Martin-in-the-Fields in London, the Arlington Street Church was the first public building constructed in Back Bay. It was dedicated in 1861. Between 1898 and 1933, sixteen Tiffany

greenpatriot

The Thomas Cass Memorial in the Public Garden at Boylston Street near Arlington Street honors an Irish immigrant who became a successful businessman and formed the 9th Massachusetts Volunteers, an Irish Regiment that fought in the Civil War. He was mortally wounded at the Battle of Malvern Hill and returned to Boston, where he died in 1862.

oldmasters

The Copley Society, 175 Newbury Street, is America's oldest nonprofit art association.

windows were installed. They display some of the company's unusual techniques, such as using multiple layers of opalescent glass to achieve shades of color. The nave underwent extensive restoration in 2001, interrupting the usual visiting schedule. It's only open reliably for the Sunday worship service at 11:00 A.M., when you'll hear the sonorous choir of sixteen bells still rung by hand. For other visiting times, call (617) 536–7050 or visit www.ascboston.org. Take note of the heroic-size bronze statue across Arlington Street from the front of the church. It shows one of the prominent Unitarian leaders and social reformers of the nineteenth century, Boston's own William Ellery Channing.

Sound rather than sight is the leading attraction around the corner at *Emmanuel Church of Boston* at 15 Newbury Street.

mug-shots

The Newbury Street mural at the corner of Newbury and Dartmouth Streets was painted in 1991. Among the seventy-two portraits of the famous and the obscure are John Winthrop, Alexander Graham Bell, John Harvard, Edgar Allen Poe, Fred Allen, and "King" Camp Gillette, inventor of the safety razor.

Since 1969 this Episcopal congregation's chorus and orchestra have performed the J. S. Bach cantata cycle as a part of the liturgy every Sunday

Flamboyancy in Stone

Five streets up Commonwealth Avenue, at the corner of Hereford Street, the **Burrage House** (314 Commonwealth Avenue) represents a kind of architectural ostentation that is rare in Boston. Built in 1889 for corporate lawyer and executive Albert Cameron Burrage, the house is virtually encrusted with ornamentation in French Gothic and early Renaissance styles. The front entrance alone sports crouching chimeras, dragon heads, and cherubs. The Hereford Street side is covered with gargoyles, demonic faces, more dragons and chimeras, even more winged cherubs, and enough snakes to drive Saint Patrick to distraction. Burrage had a knack for being out of step with his contemporaries. He ran several Boston-area gaslight companies when most Bostonians were switching to electricity, and he joined the Amalgamated Copper Company just as the federal government under Theodore Roosevelt began breaking up such giant trusts. Today his house is luxury condominiums.

light in the windows

The Hotel Vendôme, at the corner of Commonwealth Avenue and Dartmouth Street in Back Bay, was the first building in Boston with electric lights. It was built in 1871 and electrified in 1882.

between September and mid-April, twice completing the entire liturgical cycle of Bach's 194 sacred cantatas. Sunday services are at 10:00 A.M. Call (617) 536–3355.

Just half a block up the street, the Presbyterian **Church of the Covenant** at 67 Newbury Street also holds 10:00 A.M. Sunday services—the only dependable time to view the extraordinary 1890s Tiffany interior, featuring twenty-two stained-glass windows as well as an elaborate Tiffany lantern made of brass, gold paint, and layered stained glass. The lantern originally graced the Tiffany Chapel at the 1893 Chicago World's Fair. Call (617) 266–7480 or visit www.churchofthe covenant.org.

The Gothic Revival Church of the Covenant building complex serves many purposes, offering a soup kitchen and a day shelter for homeless women. On the Newbury Street side, also at number 67, you'll find the entrance to one of Newbury Street's more unusual and refreshing art galleries, **Gallery Naga.** The focus is local, with dynamic work by Boston and New England painters, sculptors, and furniture makers. The gallery is open Tuesday

soup's on

Fannie Merrit Farmer's school of cookery (founded in 1902) was located for many years at 40 Hereford Street. The 1886 mansion is now condominiums.

through Saturday 10:00 A.M. to 5:30 P.M., closed Sunday and Monday. Call (617) 267–9060 or visit www.gallerynaga.com.

Newbury Street's buildings were mostly constructed as private residences but have long housed commercial concerns. One of the finer older town houses at 99–101 Newbury Street maintains a family connection of sorts. The **New England Historic Genealogical Society,** entered at 99 Newbury Street, has more than 200,000 genealogical books as well as a wealth of other research materials and a very helpful staff.

rhymed couplet

In 1953 poets Robert Lowell and Elizabeth Hardwick purchased 239 Marlborough Street.

On the first Wednesday of every month from noon to 1:00 P.M. and again from 6:00 to 7:00 P.M., you can take advantage of the free "Getting Started" program to take a peek inside and pick up tips and techniques for beginning your family research. Once you've gone through the program, the Society provides you with a free one-day pass to start digging. The Society is open Tuesday through Saturday

9:00 A.M. to 4:45 P.M., open to 8:45 P.M. on Wednesday. It is also open until 8:45 P.M. on Thursdays from April to November. Call (617) 536–5740 or visit www. newenglandancestors.org. The annual membership fee of $60 includes free admission; a nonmember day pass is $15.

If you turn right onto Clarendon Street and walk toward Commonwealth past the "Church of the Holy Bean Blowers" (thanks to trumpeting angels on the bell tower, the First Baptist Church will always be known by this nickname), you can cross the Commonwealth Avenue mall and continue to one of the least explored residential streets of Back Bay, Marlborough Street.

Near the corner of Berkeley Street, the *French Library & Cultural Center* at 53 Marlborough Street was built as a private home in 1867. Legend has it that the salon is modeled on the Empress Josephine's private parlor at Malmaison, though nowadays it's mostly used for French language classes and small social gatherings. (It's on the left as you enter.) French culture has always had a strong foothold in Boston, and this is the second-largest private French library in the United States. The institution hosts concerts, lectures, art exhibits, cinema nights (for cine club members and their guests only), wine-and-cheese tastings, cooking classes, and, of course, language classes. It also boasts a fine children's library of French books. The $50 membership confers borrowing privileges, reduced admissions to classes and events, and admission to the cine club, but curious visitors are more than welcome to sit down with a copy of *Paris Match* in the upstairs library and enjoy a little civilized ambience. The French Library is open Tuesday

Vive la France

Since 1975 the French Library and Cultural Center has thrown one of the best parties of the summer to celebrate French independence. The **Bastille Day Street Dance Festival** takes over Marlborough Street between Berkeley and Clarendon on the Friday, Saturday, or Sunday nearest July 14 for music, a street fair, and table after table of food and drink. When darkness falls a band takes the stage and the revelry goes on until the 11:30 P.M. curfew. (This is a residential neighborhood, after all.) Tickets cost $20 in advance, $25 at the door (food and beverages additional).

withouta trace

The redoubtable Isabella Stewart Gardner is best remembered for her Venetian palazzo in the Fenway, but as a young bride she lived at 152 Beacon Street, where she began collecting art and where John Singer Sargent painted her portrait. When she sold the house to move to the Fenway in 1902, she specified that the house number (152) never be used again on Beacon Street.

through Thursday 10:00 A.M. to 8:00 P.M., Friday and Saturday 10:00 A.M. to 5:00 P.M., and for special events. Closed Sunday and Monday. For information call (617) 912–0400.

If you'd like to see the interior of one of these fine Victorian homes as people really lived in them, walk down Berkeley Street to Beacon and make a right. The **Gibson House Museum** will be on your right at 137 Beacon Street. The building was one of the most modern of its day when widow Catherine Hammond Gibson moved in with her son in 1860—it boasted gas lighting, indoor plumbing (in the basement), and a coal furnace for central heat. Catherine's grandson Charles Hammond Jr. was a famous eccentric and bon vivant and in 1936 began roping off the rooms to preserve the house as he remembered it growing up. When he would throw one of his famous bath-tub gin parties, guests were reduced to sitting on the stairs. Admission is $5.00. Tours are given on the hour between 1:00 and 3:00 P.M. Wednesday through Sunday from May through October, Saturday and Sunday from November through April. Call (617) 267–6338.

To peek inside just one more Back Bay manse, continue down Beacon to Arlington Street, turn right, and proceed to Commonwealth Avenue. Just a few buildings up on the right, the **Boston Center for Adult Education** has occupied 5 Commonwealth Avenue since 1941. The home was constructed in 1904 for industrialist Walter C. Baylies, and his family lived here until 1936. The elegant common rooms on the first floor have never been altered. The prize is the Curtis Ballroom, built in 1913 for Baylies' daughter's debut and vaguely modeled on the Petit Trianon at Versailles. The full-blown Louis XV style includes crystal chandeliers, a marble fireplace, and hand-rubbed gold leaf over the ivory paint. The building is open Monday through Thursday 9:00 A.M. to 7:00 P.M., Friday 9:00 A.M. to 5:00 P.M., closed Saturday and Sunday. If there's no class going on, you can simply walk briskly past the desk and turn left to see the ballroom. Call (617) 267–4430.

If you continue walking up Commonwealth Avenue past the Burrage House (earlier this chapter), you'll come to **Orpheus Performing Arts Treasures** in the basement level of the town house at 362 Commonwealth Avenue. This small shop buys and sells LPs and CDs, along with videos and laser discs. But it is most noted for its music, film, and theater memorabilia, including seventy-five years of playbills from some of Boston's grand old theaters. Orpheus is open Monday through Saturday from 11:00 A.M. to 8:00 P.M. and Sunday from noon to 7:00 P.M. Call (617) 247–7200.

At the end of the block, you'll reach Massachusetts Avenue, the dividing line between Back Bay and the Fenway. Turn left and it's only a short stroll to 200 Massachusetts Avenue, where the entrance to the new *Mary Baker Eddy Library for the Betterment of Humanity* is marked by a small fountain and benches that provide a quiet resting spot on the edge of the large campus of the Christian Science Center. The centerpiece of the new exhibits is the Mapparium, the 30-foot-diameter walk-through globe, built of stained glass in 1935. Its political boundaries are still fixed at that year, but a sound-and-light program updates world history, noting for example, that in 1935 only 20 percent of the world was democratic, as compared with 75 percent today. Other exhibits explore the life of Eddy, the founder of the Christian Science Church, and use her example to emphasize the power of one person to make a difference in the world. Be sure to take a peek through a glass wall to watch the newsroom of the *Christian Science Monitor* in action. Mrs. Eddy was eighty-seven years old when she started the newspaper. The library's new Quotes Café is a quiet place for a sandwich or a snack. The library is open Tuesday through Friday from 10:00 A.M. to 9:00 P.M., Saturday from 10:00 A.M. to 5:00 P.M., and Sunday from 11:00 A.M. to 5:00 P.M. Admission is $5.00. The cafe is open Tuesday through Sunday from 11:30 A.M. to 8:00 P.M. and Sunday from 11:30 A.M. to 5:00 P.M. For information call (617) 450–7000. The Christian Science basilica is noted for its organ (later this chapter).

Kenmore and the Fenway

Remember the year: 1889. That was when landscape architect Frederick Law Olmsted's innovative plan to tame the smelly swamps of the Back Bay Fens was finally in place and former swampland beyond Back Bay suddenly became prime real estate. Development of the streets around Kenmore Square and the Fenway took another two decades, resulting in a mix of striking late Victorian architecture and some pretty humdrum industrial-looking buildings. Boston University's sudden growth in the 1960s further altered the landscape, turning much of outer Commonwealth Avenue into a modern linear campus.

To begin a tour of this area, take any of the B, C, or D trains on the Green Line to Kenmore Square and exit on the Beacon Street side. At the corner beneath the landmark CITGO sign, turn right on Deerfield Street and proceed 1 block to *Bay State Road,* a Boston Architectural Conservation District dotted with prime examples of various turn-of-the-twentieth-century revival styles.

If you look to the right at the intersection, you'll see the former Sheraton Hotel at 91 Bay State Road. Boston University (BU) purchased the building in 1953 and converted it to the **Shelton Hall** dormitory. Earlier that year, New York–born playwright Eugene O'Neill died at the hotel, reportedly muttering "Born in a hotel room and, goddamn it, died in a hotel room." At the time he was visiting his Boston doctor for treatment for Parkinson's disease.

As you stroll up Bay State Road admiring the architecture, you can turn right on the dead-end Sherborn Street to reach a **pedestrian bridge over Storrow Drive** that brings you to the **Charles River Embankment,** the long riverbank park that stretches 7 miles between the Watertown and Charles River dams. Jogging and bicycle paths cross here, and there's a small picnic area. During warm weather, BU students often avail themselves of the grass for sunning, earning the area the nickname "BU Beach."

For a return to the madding crowd, follow Sherborn Street back to Commonwealth Avenue and turn right to visit Boston University's **Coit Observatory** in the College of Arts and Sciences at 725 Commonwealth Avenue. The astronomy department is located on the fifth floor and the observatory on the sixth. Posted in glass cases on the walls are some remarkable photographs taken at this optical observatory, including some hauntingly beautiful lunar eclipses. Weather permitting, the observatory welcomes visitors for sky watching on Wednesday evenings at 7:30 P.M. from October to March and at 8:30 P.M. from April to September. Call (617) 353–2630.

Farther up on Commonwealth Avenue, you'll come to the splendid Marsh

Farther-Flung BU

The Boston University campus thins out beyond the BU Bridge, but two highlights might interest you. The **Boston University Gallery,** in the School for the Arts building at 855 Commonwealth Avenue, is one of the city's most thoughtful galleries of contemporary art, often exhibiting (and initiating) traveling shows. It's free and open Tuesday through Friday 10:00 A.M. to 5:00 P.M., Saturday and Sunday 1:00 to 5:00 P.M. Call (617) 353–3329.

If you turn right at Babcock Street and walk toward the river, you come upon BU's Nickerson Field. From 1915 to 1952 it was known as **Braves Field,** home of the Boston (now Atlanta) Braves baseball team. It was the site of three World Series, the 1936 All-Star Game, and what still stands as Major League baseball's longest game: a twenty-six-inning 1-to-1 tie between the Braves and the Brooklyn Dodgers on May 1, 1920.

See the Light

If you walk behind Fenway Park and follow Ipswich Street to the left, you'll come to the **Fenway Studios** at 30 Ipswich Street, the oldest surviving structure in the United States specifically designed and still used for artists' residences and studios. The building goes back to 1905 and has been designated a National Historic Landmark. Note the immense windows that face into the shadowless north light. The artists sometimes hold an open house at their studios on one weekend in the fall. Call (617) 596–3756.

Chapel Plaza, one of BU's more spacious public spaces. Front and center is an abstract **sculpture of a flock of doves** lifting into flight by Sergio Castillo to honor Martin Luther King Jr., Nobel laureate and one of the distinguished alumni of the School of Theology.

Small portions of the **Boston University Special Collections,** one of Boston's hidden treasures, are displayed in Mugar Memorial Library at 771 Commonwealth Avenue. (The library is located behind other buildings, off the street.) As you enter, the display room on the left holds changing exhibitions, usually highlighting the life and professional career of a celebrity. The dedicated room on the right is jammed with show-business memorabilia, including Fred Astaire's dance shoes, Gene Kelly's Oscar for *An American in Paris,* and original drawings of the comic strips *Dennis the Menace, Little Orphan Annie,* and *Li'l Abner.* Portions of the Bette Davis collection are also on display. Davis, who grew up in nearby Somerville and Newton, contributed 119,000 documents, including her school report cards, 111 scrapbooks, and her leatherbound copy of the script for *All About Eve.* These rooms are open Monday through Friday 9:00 A.M. to 4:30 P.M. Additional cases on the library's main floor exhibit some of the rare books and manuscripts from the collections—items such as early editions of books by Dante, Galileo, Cervantes, and Diderot. You can peruse these during the library's usual hours: Monday through Thursday 8:00 A.M. to midnight, Friday and Saturday 8:00 A.M. to 11:00 P.M., Sunday 10:00 A.M. to midnight. Admission is free.

The **Photographic Resource Center (PRC)** at 832 Commonwealth Avenue is Boston's gathering spot for photographers and lovers of photography. The PRC hosts stimulating, sometimes-controversial exhibitions of contemporary photography. The center is open Tuesday through Friday 10:00 A.M. to 6:00 P.M., Thursday noon to 8:00 P.M., Saturday and Sunday noon to 5:00 P.M. Admission is $3.00, $2.00 seniors and students, free to BU community at all times and to everyone on Thursday. Call (617) 975–0600.

If you walk back to the awkward main intersection of Kenmore Square, you

no stones thrown

There are 10,344 identical panes of glass in the John Hancock Tower. At 790 feet, it is the tallest building in New England.

can make your way over to the Fenway. The *Hotel Buckminster,* at 645 Beacon Street on the point of the square, looms large in the darkest annals of baseball history. It was here that Boston bookie Joe Sullivan made a deal with Chicago White Sox first baseman Chick Gandil—a solid .280 hitter—to throw the 1919 World Series in what became known as the Black Sox Scandal. Gandil was one of eight Chicago players banned forever from organized baseball. Also among the outcasts was the legendary "Shoeless" Joe Jackson, who played his heart out in the series but refused to rat out his teammates.

Before crossing Beacon, you might want to walk up a block to visit the *Art Institute of Boston* at 700 Beacon Street, a 562-student school in Kenmore Square overwhelmed by behemoth Boston University. The gallery in the ground-floor lobby maintains a strong schedule of traveling exhibitions, often emphasizing art in craft media and folk art from around the world. The gallery is open Monday through Saturday 9:00 A.M. to 6:00 P.M., Sunday noon to 5:00 P.M. Call (617) 262–1223 or visit www.aiboston.edu.

Although the future of the oldest baseball park in the major leagues still remains in question, new owners of the Red Sox have made *Fenway Park* much more welcoming to visitors with more seats, renovated bathrooms, and a wider range of food choices in an expanded concourse. Fans pack the seats for home games, but surprisingly few ever bother to see the ballpark behind the scenes. Tours include the press box, broadcast booth, and Red Sox Hall of Fame. When the field is available, fans can even walk the warning track beneath the Green Monster. John Updike said the park offers "a compromise between man's Euclidian determinations and Nature's beguiling irregularities."

Decide for yourself. Tours run April through September daily from 9:00 A.M. to 4:00 P.M. or until three hours before game time, whichever is earlier. Admission is $9.00 for adults. Call (617) 236–6666 or visit boston.red sox.mlb.com.

The safest transit into the Back Bay Fens, one of the less frequently visited parks of the

big sounds

The Christian Science basilica at 175 Huntington Avenue has the largest organ in the Western Hemisphere, with 13,290 pipes. It was built by the Aeolian-Skinner Company of Boston and is played at Sunday 10:00-A.M. and Wednesday-noon services.

Lourdes of the North

The ***Basilica of Our Lady of Perpetual Help*** at 1545 Tremont Street is that Romanesque, cathedral-like church rising atop Mission Hill not far from Harvard Medical School. The church was built as a Redemptorist Fathers mission to the Roman Catholic immigrants to Boston between 1871 and 1874. Its 250-foot bell towers were added in 1910, and in 2001 the church was completely restored. Massive pink-and-gray marble columns support arched ceilings that rise more than seven stories. Stained-glass windows depict the life of Jesus, while the walls and cupola are covered with Byzantine-style murals and frescoes. What draws people to the basilica, however, is the Perpetual Help Shrine. The first miracle of the shrine is said to have occurred in 1883 when a young woman whose spine was shattered was able to walk again. Indeed, the altar is flanked by cast-aside crutches. The healing service on Sundays at 4:00 P.M. is the most popular. The church is open for visitors daily from 7:00 A.M. to 7:00 P.M.; enter through the rectory after 1:00 P.M. Call (617) 445–2600; themissionchurch.com.

Emerald Necklace, is to walk past Fenway Park on Yawkey Way, which becomes Jersey Street as it crosses Boylston Street. At the end of Jersey Street, you can stroll across a short crosswalk and enter the Fens at one of their most glorious spots. Straight ahead of you is the rear of the Museum of Fine Arts, a model of classicism through the trees. On your left is the entrance to the ***James P. Kelleher Rose Garden.*** Looming behind it are the Prudential and Hancock towers of Back Bay. This display garden, at its best during June and July, has benches for contemplation among the heady blooms.

By following the path through the Fens toward the Museum of Fine Arts, you'll spot the entrance to the ***School of the Museum of Fine Arts*** on the corner of Museum Road at 230 The Fenway. Here's an opportunity to sample eclectic art exhibitions by students and faculty at the Grossman Gallery, inside the front entrance on the right. Admission is free and the gallery is open Monday, Tuesday, Wednesday, Friday, and Saturday 10:00 A.M. to 5:00 P.M., and Thursday 10:00 A.M. to 8:00 P.M. Call (617) 267–6100.

Hardly more than a flick of the brush away, the ***Massachusetts College of Art***—best known as MassArt—is the nation's only freestanding state-supported art college, dating from 1873, when prescient legislators realized that a college of art and design was a key asset in maintaining the state's economic preeminence. The exhibition program in MassArt's Huntington and Bakalar galleries in the South Building mixes avant-garde art and exhibitions with strong social themes. Admission is free. MassArt's South Building is at the corner of Huntington and Longwood Avenues and the galleries are open

Monday through Friday 10:00 A.M. to 6:00 P.M., Saturday 11:00 A.M. to 5:00 P.M., closed Sunday. Call (617) 879–7333 or visit www.massart.edu.

Persevere another few blocks out Huntington Avenue from MassArt to visit the **Warren Anatomical Museum,** which is located in the Harvard Medical area's Francis A. Countway Library. The library stands directly behind the large number "677" on a pole at Huntington Avenue next to the Harvard School of Public Health. Not for the squeamish, this collection of medical rarities (including delicate and rather beautiful skeletons of conjoined twins who died at birth, examples of arthritic bone disfiguration, and many other dried specimens) is located on the fifth floor of the library. The museum was founded in 1847 from the private holdings of Dr. John Collins Warren (1778–1856), who began collecting the specimens while he was a medical student in London. Admission is free. Visitors must sign in at the front desk. The library (at 10 Shattuck Street, but actually embedded within the Harvard Medical School campus) is open Monday through Thursday 8:00 A.M. to 11:00 P.M., Friday 8:00 A.M. to 7:00 P.M., Saturday 9:00 A.M. to 5:00 P.M., and Sunday noon to 11:00 P.M. The fifth-floor museum is open Monday through Friday 9:00 A.M. to 5:00 P.M. Call (617) 432–6196.

Within the same complex, the menu at **Sebastian's Café** was developed by nutritionists from the Harvard School of Public Health and is dedicated to the proposition that healthy food can also be tasty and filling. Even with reduced salt and fat, cooks turn out such tempting fare as vegetarian pad Thai; chicken with mango juice, hot peppers, and cilantro; and salmon braised in wine and fresh dill. For the nutritionally reluctant, there's even a whole-wheat pizza. The cafe is open Monday through Thursday 7:00 A.M. to 4:00 P.M. and Friday 7:00 A.M. to 3:00 P.M. Call (617) 432–1045.

From the Medical School, take the first opportunity to cross busy Huntington Avenue at a "walk" light and set out purposefully toward the distant towers of Back Bay. If you begin to flag, take an inbound Green Line train and get off at Forsyth Street by the Northeastern University Physical Education Center, better known as Cabot Cage. There's a plaque noting that the Huntington Avenue wall was the left field line of the **Huntington Avenue Grounds,** a baseball park constructed in 1901 for the Boston Pilgrims of the American League (later the Boston Red Sox). If you walk around on the other side of Cabot Cage, you'll see a bronze statue of the greatest pitcher of all times, Cy Young, staring at a piece of granite shaped like home plate some 60 feet and 6 inches away. This was the exact site of the first World Series, a best-of-nine-games affair that opened on October 1, 1903. For the record, the Pilgrims, behind Young's pitching (he won twenty-eight games in 1903), won the series in eight games over the National League representatives, the Pittsburgh Pirates. General admission to the Series was 50 cents. The following year, Young pitched the first perfect game of the twentieth century here.

Places to Stay in Back Bay and the Fenway

Colonnade Hotel,
120 Huntington Avenue;
(617) 424–7000 or
(800) 962–3030;
www.colonnadehotel.com.
Favored by the better bus tours, the Colonnade also does a brisk trade with European business travelers. In the summer it has the city's only outdoor rooftop pool, and it's handy to shopping at Copley Place. Moderate to expensive.

Fairmont Copley Plaza Hotel,
138 St. James Street;
(617) 267–5300 or
(800) 441–1414;
www.fairmont.com.
It's hard to fault the glamour of this magisterial hotel, with its stunning lobby and public areas, cozy rooms, and graceful and open suites. It was good enough for Richard Burton and Elizabeth Taylor, after all. Expensive.

The Gryphon House,
9 Bay State Road;
(617) 375–9003 or
(877) 375–9003;
www.innboston.com.
One of the earliest brownstone mansions on Bay State Road (built in 1895), the Gryphon House's eight rooms are nearly the size of studio apartments. They're all furnished in late-Victorian style and feature working gas fireplaces, wet bars, and high-speed Internet access. Moderate to expensive.

Lenox Hotel,
710 Boylston Street;
(617) 536–5300 or
(800) 225–7676;
www.lenoxhotel.com.
Freshly renovated, this circa-1900 Copley Square landmark has made a triumphant return to luxury status. The large corner rooms have working fireplaces. Expensive.

Midtown Motor Hotel,
220 Huntington Avenue;
(617) 262–1000 or
(800) 343–1177;
www.midtownhotel.com.
You'll look far and wide to

AUTHORS' FAVORITES IN BACK BAY AND FENWAY

Boston Public Library Rare Book Room

Trinity Church bookstore

Emmanuel Church services with Bach cantatas

New England Historic Genealogical Society

Coit Observatory

Boston University Special Collections

Huntington and Bakalar galleries, Massachusetts College of Art

find such large rooms so handy to Back Bay. The recent complete renovation has brought this older in-town motel back up to snuff. Free parking. Moderate.

Newbury Guest House,
261 Newbury Street; (617) 437–7666 or (800) 437–7668; www.hagopianhotels.com. This group of Back Bay dwellings has been connected on the interior to create somewhat spartan but perfectly adequate B&B lodgings at Back Bay's best price. Inexpensive to moderate.

Places to Eat in Back Bay and the Fenway

Betty's Wok & Noodle Diner,
250 Huntington Avenue; (617) 424–1950.
Located across Huntington Avenue from Symphony Hall, Betty's is just plain fun—as if it were an American diner in China. You design the dinner by picking rice or noodles, chicken or vegetables, and a sauce for the entree. Top it off with a wedge of old-fashioned chocolate layer cake. Open Tuesday through Thursday noon to 10:00 P.M., Friday and Saturday noon to 11:00 P.M., Sunday noon to 10:00 P.M. Inexpensive.

Boston Beer Works,
61 Brookline Avenue; (617) 536–BEER.
Across from Fenway Park, this brewpub serves better-than-average pub grub. Two people can stuff themselves on a single plate of barbecued ribs, andouille sausage, chicken, and steak tips. Of course, you'll need beer with that. Open daily 11:30 A.M. to 1:00 A.M. Inexpensive.

Brasserie Jo,
Colonnade Hotel, 120 Huntington Avenue; (617) 425–3240.
The Alsatian brasserie is a rarity in these parts, making it fun to visit Jo for steak-frites and a liter of Alsatian pilsner. Sometimes convention-goers from nearby hotels can stretch the wait staff too thin, so have patience. Open Monday through Friday 6:30 A.M. to 11:00 P.M., Saturday 7:00 A.M. to 11:00 P.M., Sunday 7:00 A.M. to 10:00 P.M. Moderate.

Bravo
Museum of Fine Arts 465 Huntington Avenue; (617) 369–3474
As befits its location on the second level of the MFA's West Wing, Bravo is decorated in a warm pumpkin color with whimsical lamps and fabrics providing a visual punch. Each plate that emerges from the kitchen is artfully garnished. This white-tablecloth restaurant is a good option for sophisticated dining in the Fenway, especially considering that parking in the MFA lot is free for diners after 5:30 P.M.

Open for lunch daily 11:30 A.M. to 3:00 P.M., dinner Wednesday through Friday 5:30 to 8:30 P.M. Moderate.

Brown Sugar Cafe,
129 Jersey Street; (617) 266–2928.
Located where Jersey Street meets the Fenway, Brown Sugar sets the standard for good Thai food in Boston—crunchy veggies, subtle sauces, no MSG. You might even run into Steven Tyler of the band Aerosmith—it's one of his favorite places to eat. Open Monday through Thursday 11:00 A.M. to 10:00 P.M., Friday and Saturday 11:00 A.M. to 11:00 P.M., Sunday noon to 10:00 P.M. Inexpensive.

Buteco Brazilian Cafe,
130 Jersey Street; (617) 247–9508.
Right across the street from Brown Sugar, Buteco features Brazilian home cooking in the Africa-tinged style of the Bahia province. On the weekend, join Brazilian families savoring their national dish of *feijoada,* a stew of black beans with pork, sausage, and dried beef served with rice, collard greens, and fresh orange segments. Open Monday through Thursday noon to 10:00 P.M., Friday noon to 11:00 P.M., Saturday 3:00 to 11:00 P.M., Sunday 3:00 to 10:00 P.M. Inexpensive.

Ciao Bella,
240A Newbury Street; (617) 536–2626.
The prime location (at the corner of Newbury and Fairfield Streets) makes Ciao Bella a place to be seen

AUTHORS' FAVORITE PLACES TO EAT IN BACK BAY AND FENWAY

Betty's Wok & Diner	Oak Room (Fairmont Copley Plaza)
Bravo	Parish Cafe

during the alfresco-dining season. The old-fashioned Italian comfort food (minestrone, chicken Parmesan, fettuccine Alfredo) is for diners who like to recognize what's on their plates. Many Boston jocks, including shortstop Nomar Garciaparra, often hang out here. Open Sunday to Wednesday 11:30 A.M. to 11:00 P.M., Thursday through Saturday 11:30 A.M. to 11:30 P.M. Moderate.

Oak Room,
Fairmont Copley
Plaza Hotel,
138 St. James Avenue;
(617) 267–5300.
See page 39 for full description.

Parish Cafe,
361 Boylston Street;
(617) 247–4777.
The house specialties are sandwiches designed by some of Boston's leading chefs, including Lydia (Biba) Shire's lobster salad on

pepper brioche. American classics are also strong—for example, good old meat loaf with brown gravy and garlic mashed potatoes. Tables outside on the street disappear quickly in the summer. Open Monday through Saturday 11:30 A.M. to 1:00 A.M., Sunday noon to 1:00 A.M. Inexpensive to moderate.

Pho Pasteur,
119 Newbury Street;
(617) 262–8200.
This Back Bay branch of the Vietnamese soup restaurant chain that began in Chinatown is small and cozy and an incredible value. Noodle soups (pho) are always a good bet at Pho Pasteur, but some of more traditional Vietnamese entrees (caramelized sliced catfish in a casserole or "pork with vegetable") make sensational light eating. Open daily 11:00 A.M. to 10:00 P.M. Inexpensive.

Stephanie's on Newbury,
190 Newbury Street;
(617) 236-0990.
Chef-owner Stephanie Siddell knows that comfort food never goes out of style, so she piles it on: a tenderloin steak the size of a baseball for meat lovers, cornucopia-size salads for weight watchers, a soothing chicken pot pie for anyone who needs a little mothering. The summer sidewalk is festive, but when the weather chills, there's a warm fireplace between the dining room and bar. Fruit salad might sound like an odd meal, but with no grapes and no apples as fillers, it's a riot of color and explosive taste, topped with yogurt and freshly toasted granola. Open Monday through Saturday 11:30 A.M. to midnight, Sunday 10:00 A.M. to midnight. Moderate.

Charlestown, North End, and East Boston

Boston's northern neighborhoods are united principally by their enduring sense of ethnicity, a legacy of the massive Irish and Italian migrations at the end of the nineteenth and beginning of the twentieth centuries and the Latin American and Southeast Asian immigration of more recent years. While the North End is a famous visitor attraction in its own right, even Bostonians often regard "Eastie" as a place to pass through when going to and from the airport. Charlestown represents that piece of the Freedom Trail that falls prey to tourism triage when travelers weigh the number of sights they want to see against their remaining hours. Yet all three neighborhoods sit directly on Boston Harbor, and each offers its own colloquial experience of the city.

Charlestown

Before there was Boston, there was Charlestown. In 1629 ten Puritan families and their servants left overcrowded Salem and settled on a marshy peninsula between the mouths of the Charles and Mystic Rivers. They called their community Charlestown. Even as these residents dug in for the winter, John Winthrop and a group of wealthy and influential Puritans

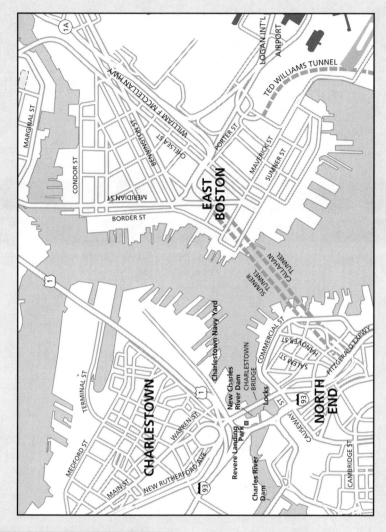

EAST BOSTON

CHARLESTOWN

NORTH END

LOGAN INT'L AIRPORT

TED WILLIAMS TUNNEL

CALLAHAN TUNNEL

SUMNER TUNNEL

Charlestown Navy Yard

New Charles River Dam

CHARLESTOWN BRIDGE

Locks

Revere Landing Park

Charles River Dam

MARGINAL ST

CONDOR ST

BENNINGTON ST

CHELSEA ST

WILLIAM F. MCCLELLAN HWY

PORTER ST

MAVERICK ST

SUMNER ST

MERIDIAN ST

BORDER ST

TERMINAL ST

MEDFORD ST

MAIN ST

WARREN ST

NEW RUTHERFORD AVE

COMMERCIAL ST

SALEM ST

HANOVER ST

FITZGERALD EXPWY

CAUSEWAY ST

CAMBRIDGE ST

1A

11

1

1

93

93

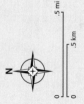

N

0 .5 mi

0 .5 km

still in England purchased controlling interest in the land grant that included Charlestown. Lo and behold, the next summer Winthrop and nearly a thousand other colonists anchored in the harbor off the peninsula, and the first Charlestownites (they call themselves "Townies" these days) were swamped by the newcomers.

rising in the east

In the 1830s the marshes between five islands were filled to create East Boston. Mansions were built on wide boulevards and were marketed as a getaway for wealthy Bostonians. The area was accessible only by ferry.

Their fragile infrastructure was also swamped. The demand on the freshwater spring was so extreme that salt water began to seep in, and the primitive sewage arrangements and preponderance of mosquitoes led to widespread disease. Residents were afflicted with everything from typhus to "hectic fever," a generalized malaise that seems to have been a combination of poor nutrition, exposure, and the aftereffects of long weeks at sea. When hermit William Blaxton invited Winthrop and his band to the Shawmut peninsula, Winthrop moved his followers lock, stock, and barrel across the Charles River, leaving the Townies to their fate. But before the Bostonians departed, they erected the first Great House of the Massachusetts Bay Colony, held the first formal worship services, and set Boston history in motion—all in Charlestown. The two communities would remain apart for more than two centuries, until Charlestown voted to join the city of Boston in 1873.

cheaper by the yard

In 1801 the U.S. Navy paid $39,214 for forty-three acres in Charlestown to build a Navy yard.

Colonial Charlestown was almost entirely leveled by British cannon during the American Revolution, so most of what you see today dates from the nineteenth century and later. But surprising reminders of its earliest days persist. Newly reclaimed *City Square,* accessible by bus from Haymarket on the Orange and Green MBTA Lines, is the best place to begin exploring.

Now a gateway park to Charlestown, City Square marks the spot where the first Puritans set up the town in 1629. But even the Puritans weren't the first inhabitants. From at least 1000 B.C., the indigenous peoples of New England came here to dig clay and fire it into pottery. In fact, some archaeologists believe that the little plot has been continuously visited, and perhaps even inhabited, for the last 10,000 years. After decades as a wasteland between awkward highway connections, City Square was transformed into a park in the 1990s. A stylish fountain stands at the center, topped with a herring weather vane. Water flows from the mouths of cod—the original staple of the entire Massachusetts Bay Colony. Relief sculptures depict cod skeletons being used to fertilize corn.

Cod Sculptures, City Square

When you walk around on the grass, you'll see fieldstones and lines of concrete that show the original outline of the Great House. Circles of concrete indicate the corner posts found by archaeologists when the plot was excavated in the 1980s. Soon after Winthrop (and thus the government) moved over to Boston proper, the Great House was no longer needed for community and government activities. It became the Three Cranes Tavern and was expanded several times before its demise in 1775, when it burned during the Battle of Bunker Hill. But the outlines are very clear, showing the post holes, doors, and hearth and the main tavern room above the wine cellar. Additional excavations for highway construction turned up some of the original Charlestown privies, which were as much refuse dumps as outhouses. Among the contents were pieces of imported pottery, fine wine glasses, and the bones of butchered animals—all indicators that the colonists were hardly a deprived, impoverished lot.

hexed

The first person to be executed for witch-craft in America was Margaret Jones, who was hanged in Charlestown in 1648.

Behind City Square and rising from the divided highway is Town Hill, where Governor Winthrop instructed the colonists to build a pallisaded fort. Today the area is walled off as *John Harvard Mall*, in honor of the young "sometimes minister of God's word" who died of consumption in Charlestown in 1638, a scant fourteen months after coming from England. His will donated all of his books and half his estate (800 pounds sterling) to the fledgling college in nearby Cambridge, which Winthrop and the residents promptly renamed Harvard College. (See "Cambridge" chapter.)

Several plaques and a central monument recount local history at great, if not always revealing, length. One plaque proclaims "this low mound of earth the memorial of a mighty nation," while another notes that the "first public worship of God" by the Massachusetts Bay colonists took place on this hill "under a great oak." And so the First Church in Boston was born. (The spiritual descendants of that congregation now worship at 66 Marlborough Street in Back Bay.)

firstlady

A plaque on the left wall of the Revere Mall in the North End honors Ann Pollard (1620–1725), likely the first European woman to come ashore in Boston. She landed with Governor John Winthrop at the foot of today's Prince Street—and lived to be 105.

If you exit the Mall at the top of the hill and walk right, you'll be on Harvard Street, which functions as a sort of CliffsNotes of *row house styles of the nineteenth century,* ranging from Federal through Victorian and even boasting a triple-decker or two. Near the intersection with Main Street, you'll even pass a modern housing development, cleverly disguised with generic red brick to look (at first glance) at least a century older than it is. Right at the Main Street corner stands one of the real rarities in Boston—a house built of split (not cut) stones. It dates from around 1800.

Directly across the intersection, at the corner of Main and Pleasant Streets, the **Warren Tavern** at 2 Pleasant Street is one of the oldest buildings in Charlestown. This building was constructed in 1780. It is perhaps telling that a public house was among the first buildings to go up during the reconstruction of Charlestown after it was leveled during the Revolution. The tavern was

Stones of the Forebears

Farther out Main Street, you can turn left on Phipps Street and walk to the end to reach the **Phipps Street Burying Ground,** established in 1630. The cemetery seems a little lonesome these days, as road construction has left it in an isolated parcel and the City of Boston keeps the gates locked to prevent vandalism. For admission, call the Boston Parks Department at (617) 635–4505. The earliest stones here date from the 1640s, and connoisseurs of cemetery art prize these grounds for the work of the anonymous Charlestown Carver, one of Boston's first mortuary artists. This master craftsman set the style for younger artisans, establishing the basic vocabulary of imagery used for the next two centuries. His death's heads often have eyebrows that end in uplifted curlicues. Some other examples of his work are found in the more easily visited Granary and Copp's Hill Burying Grounds in Downtown and the North End, respectively.

named for Dr. Joseph Warren, who served as president of the Massachusetts Provincial Congress in 1774, a general in the Massachusetts Army, and a member of the Committee of Correspondence, the cell of patriots who organized the Revolution. Despite his rank in the provincial forces, Warren volunteered to serve as a private in the Continental Army and was killed at the Battle of Bunker Hill. The tavern had its ups and downs over the ensuing centuries, and was derelict and scheduled for demolition when it was restored to its present state. Warren Tavern is a dependable stop for a pint and better-than-average pub fare. It's open Monday through Friday 11:15 A.M. to 10:30 P.M., Saturday and Sunday 10:30 A.M. to 10:30 P.M. Call (617) 241–8142.

Heading back from the Warren Tavern toward the North End on Warren Street, the third street on the left, Winthrop, will take you uphill to the **Charlestown parade ground,** also known on some maps as Winthrop Square or the Training Field. Now a fine park, it was set aside in 1632 as a place for the Charlestown militia to drill. Local soldiers mustered here and left for battle in 1775, in 1812, and again in 1860. When you walk up through the parade ground toward Bunker Hill Monument (very much *on* the beaten path), pause to read the plaques on the heights of the park. They list the American casualties of the Battle of Bunker Hill. The rather boisterous and buxom Victory statue within the walls of the park honors the soldiers and sailors who fought "for the preservation of the Union."

Adams Street runs along the uphill side of the parade ground. Follow it to the end to Chestnut Street and cross Chelsea Street to reach the Charlestown Navy Yard. The Navy Yard is one of the two Charlestown stops on the Freedom Trail (the other is Bunker Hill Monument), but most visitors come to see the USS *Constitution,* neglecting the USS **Cassin Young,** moored about 50 yards away. This 376-foot World War II–era destroyer is named for a Congressional Medal of Honor winner who swam back to his burning ship and rescued survivors during the Pearl Harbor attack. The *Cassin Young* survived two hits by kamikaze aircraft during the 1945 invasion of Okinawa, but twenty-three of her crew were killed and more than a hundred were wounded. Through the Cold War, the ship came to Charlestown to dock for modernization and

Hop Across the Harbor

If you're in a rush to get to the downtown waterfront, you can catch an **MBTA ferry** between the Charlestown Navy Yard and Long Wharf. The ride costs $1.25 and operates about every half-hour from 6:00 A.M. to 8:00 P.M. weekdays, 10:00 A.M. to 6:00 P.M. weekends and holidays. No service on Christmas Day and New Year's Day.

maintenance until it was decom-missioned in 1960. You can tour the main deck on your own and park rangers will take you below, where Big Band music plays in the background. Open spring and fall daily 10:00 A.M. to 4:00 P.M. with tours at 11:00 A.M., 2:00 P.M.,

goldenoldies

The bells at Old North Church are the oldest in the city. They were cast in England in 1744 and are still rung every Saturday and Sunday.

and 3:00 P.M. Open July and August daily 10:00 A.M. to 4:00 P.M. Tours every hour except noon. Call (617) 242–5652 for winter hours.

When you leave the Navy Yard, turn left on Constitution Road and follow it under the Charlestown Bridge to reach the neighborhood's newest green space, **Paul Revere Park.** Some historians speculate that Revere stood here on the night of April 17, 1775, to watch for the signal lanterns from Old North Church. Seeing two lanterns, Revere knew the British were rowing over to Charlestown behind him for their march on Lexington and Concord, and he hightailed it out of there to warn the Middlesex countryside. With the removal of the Central Artery the park has one of the best, most scenic views of the Leonard Zakim Bunker Hill Memorial Bridge. The widest cable-stay bridge ever attempted, it serves as a landmark entrance to Boston from the north.

At the end of the road through the park, you'll come to one of the marvels of modern engineering, the **Charles River Dam and Locks.** The first Charles River Dam, on the site of the Museum of Science, was built in 1908 to stop the tidal flooding of Back Bay. By the 1970s that structure had been so badly damaged by hurricanes and winter storms that the Army Corps of Engineers and the Metropolitan District Commission constructed this new dam

Good Sports

The **Sports Museum of New England,** on the fifth and sixth floors of the FleetCenter on the Charles River side of Causeway Street, displays photographs and memorabilia of great moments in New England sports. Most exhibits are devoted to the achievements of specific stars, such as hockey's Bobby Orr and baseball's Carl Yazstremski. Open Monday through Thursday 11:00 A.M. to 5:00 P.M. Admission to building on the half hour from 11:00 A.M. to 3:00 P.M. Admission is $6.00, $4.00 for seniors and ages six to seventeen. Call (617) 624–1234. The FleetCenter also offers behind-the-scenes tours of the sports complex from Memorial Day through Labor Day. Call (617) 624–1234 for weekly schedule. Admission is $6.00, $4.00 for seniors and ages six to seventeen. Call (617) 624–1500. Hours of FleetCenter and Sports Museum tours are subject to change to accommodate FleetCenter events.

a half-mile downriver. Its primary purpose is to maintain the height of the Charles River 8 feet above low tide in the harbor. Its pumping station—capable of moving 3.7 million gallons of water a minute out of the river during flood conditions—keeps the Charles on an even keel. Locks in the dam allow pleasure boats to pass between the harbor and the river in a matter of minutes—everything from large sightseeing vessels to intrepid kayakers. You're allowed to walk across the locks if you stay within the guardrails. This can mean waiting while boats pass each way, but it's a fascinating process to watch. You'll come out near North Station on Causeway Street a short distance from the Charlestown Bridge, ready to tackle the North End. Rangers with the Department of Conservation and Recreation give occasional free tours of the dam and locks. Call (617) 722–5445.

North End

The North End is one of the most frequently visited neighborhoods in Boston. Old North Church, the Paul Revere House, and Copp's Hill Burying Ground—all stops on the Freedom Trail—bring millions of travelers into the area every year. The North End is packed with restaurants and bustling with street life, especially during the summer. But against all odds, it also remains a residential neighborhood, although its nineteenth-century tenement buildings have acquired many twenty-first-century amenities. Yet for all its obvious lures, the North End is like a good friend who constantly surprises you with his depth.

Whether you are coming from Charlestown (either by the bridge or over the dam and locks), or arriving by Green Line to North Station, a good place to start exploring the lesser-known parts of the North End is at the corner of Commercial and North Washington Streets on the Boston side of the Charlestown Bridge.

As you follow Commercial Street around the harbor front, you'll en-

Pepperoni, Extra Mushrooms

At 11½ Thacher Street—the corner where Thacher, North Margin, and Thacher Court converge—*Pizzeria Regina* was born. Local branches by the same name make unremarkable pies, but this original dark, atmospheric little bar ought to be a culinary landmark. Settle into one of the wooden booths and enjoy. This pizza lovers' paradise also serves wine and beer. It's open Monday through Thursday 11:00 A.M. to 11:00 P.M., Friday and Saturday 11:00 A.M. to midnight, Sunday noon to 11:00 P.M. Inexpensive. Call (617) 227–0765.

counter the seemingly unremarkable **parking garage at 600 Commercial Street,** which actually has several claims to fame. For starters, it was the site of the Brinks Job. In 1950 seven men wearing rubber masks stole $2.7 million from the armored delivery service's counting room here in the largest single cash robbery to that time. The government ended up spending $29 million to catch the crooks. The walls of the counting room have been removed, but its original tile floor remains. One of the oldest surviving parking garages in the United States (built in 1925), it was placed on the National Register of Historic Places in 1997. All four parking levels can be reached from Hull Street, which ascends a hill just east of the garage, providing access to each level as it climbs. This clever construction won the establishment a listing in *Ripley's Believe It or Not of Odd Places.*

Across Commercial Street from the parking garage, **Steriti Memorial Rink,** an ice-skating venue reopened in November 2002 after extensive renovations, which included adding two indoor bocce courts. The rink takes full advantage of its loca-

cheaphomers

Puopolo Park's two baseball fields have the shortest left and right fields in baseball because a regulation park can't be squeezed into the space between the street and the harbor.

tion on Boston's inner harbor, with wide windows that permit panoramic views while you glide along. Open late September to early June Monday through Friday 3:00 to 11:00 P.M., Saturday and Sunday 6:00 A.M. to 11:00 P.M. Call (617) 523–9327. For information on other skating rinks, call (617) 727–4708.

One of the nicest portions of the **Boston Harbor Walk** follows Commercial Street. Before you reach the U.S. Coast Guard facility on the site of Hart's Shipyard where the USS *Constitution* was built, you'll come to an area known alternately as **Puopolo Park** or **the Senator Joseph A. Langone Jr. and the Honorable Clementina Langone Recreation Complex.** (The Langones have been an influential family in the North End for nearly a century. When Langone Funeral Home laid out executed anarchists Nicola Sacco and Bartolomeo Vanzetti in August 1927, the funeral cortege stretched for blocks down Hanover Street.) By either name, the park is most popular for its three sandstone-dust **bocce courts,** where mostly older men speaking Italian toss the balls 70-plus feet with stunning finesse and athleticism. The object of the game is to see who can get their bocce ball closest to the *pallina,* or target ball. If you'd like to practice at home, Salem Street True Value Hardware at 89 Salem Street sells bocce ball sets; call (617) 523–4759.

Attention, Shoppers!

The North End is Boston's best hunting ground for authentic foods and wines of Italy. You can explore on your own—or you can hone in on the best of the best by signing up for **Michele Topor's North End Market Tour.** Topor has been teaching cooking, catering, and leading tours in the North End and in Italy since 1979. Her three-hour market tour (with lots of sampling) is offered Wednesday and Saturday at 10:00 A.M. and 2:00 P.M. and Friday at 3:00 P.M. Reservations are required. Fee is $39. Call (617) 523-6032; www.cucinare.com.

Look for the plaque in Langone Park that commemorates the site of the **Great Molasses Flood.** In January 1919 a tank holding 2.3 million gallons of molasses ruptured at the corner of Commercial and Charter Streets, sending a 50-foot wave of molasses down Commercial Street. The old saw may refer to "slower than cold molasses," but even in the dead of winter, this tidal wave of goo rolled along at an estimated thirty-five miles per hour, engulfing a hundred houses and suffocating twenty-one people. On hot summer days, some residents claim they can still smell molasses.

After you've watched a couple of rounds of bocce, climb Snowhill Street to Hull Street, which runs along the ridge of Copp's Hill behind the famous burial ground. North End dwellings are notorious for their cramped quarters, but no other can claim the distinction of 44 Hull Street as the **narrowest house in Boston.** Only about 10 feet wide, it stands three-and-a-half stories high. Local lore says it was built around 1800 to spite the neighbors in the house behind it by blocking their light and view.

Hull Street ends at Salem Street in front of the Old North Church. If you are in the neighborhood on a Wednesday afternoon from June through August, walk down the path between the church and the gift shop and past the gardens to small Unity Street. The **Clough House** at 21 Unity Street dates from about 1712 and was built by Ebenezer Clough, who is identified on a plaque as one of Boston's "substantial mechanicks." In fact, he was a master mason who worked on building Old North Church. During the summer, volunteers open his house for tours on Wednesday between 10:00 A.M. and 2:00 P.M. Donation suggested. No phone.

Back on Salem Street, the **North Bennet Street School,** at 39 North Bennet Street, sits on the next corner downhill. Established in 1881 to teach job skills to immigrants, it continues to foster some of those same forms of artisanry—carving decorative woodwork, making and repairing violins, creating reproduction furniture. The school offers study programs for certificates as well as individual classes to the community. Call (617) 227-0155.

You may be in the mood to wet your whistle in one of the famous cafes of Hanover Street. But if you'd like to rub shoulders with local North Enders, especially those of Italian descent, consider spending a Sunday evening glued to one of the two televisions at the **Corner Cafe,** 87 Prince Street on the corner of Margaret Street. Neighbors gather on Sunday nights to watch *The Sopranos* on HBO, sometimes reminiscing about similar characters who once ruled the streets of the North End. (Like the mobsters in *The Sopranos*, most Boston wise guys long ago moved to the suburbs—at least, those who didn't end up in jail or the witness protection program.) The bar food is bounteous and inexpensive, the taps pour local beers, and when the Sicilian soap isn't playing, the TVs are tuned to two different sports channels. Open Monday through Thursday 11:00 A.M. to 1:00 A.M., Friday and Saturday 11:00 A.M. to 2:00 A.M., Sunday noon to 1:00 A.M. Call (617) 523–8997.

We tend to think of lower Salem Street as a cornucopia of fine food. There isn't an hour of the day when you can't get fresh bread or pastries at **A. Bova & Sons Modern Bakery** at 134 Salem Street. Night workers from all over the city come in for post-midnight pizza slices, then stop back for hot rolls to take home to their families for breakfast. Open continuously. Call (617) 523–5601. Practically across the street, the venerable coffee roaster **Polcari** at 105 Salem Street began providing Italian-roast coffee beans to the neighborhood in 1932 and was once New England's leading supplier of espresso-grind coffee. The hauntingly atmospheric shop still sells coffee, along with a variety of herbs and spices. Open Monday through Saturday 8:30 A.M. to 5:50 P.M., closed Sunday. Call (617) 227–0786.

In keeping with the neighborhood, **Salem True Value Hardware Store,** at 89 Salem Street, sells a lot more than hammers and nails. You can select an espresso maker and a set of cups to make and serve espresso at home using the beans you just bought at Polcari. If you want to try your hand at an entire Italian feast, you can also purchase meat grinders; vegetable mills; cheese graters; pasta, ravioli, or cavatelli makers; gnocchi boards; cannoli tubes; and pizzelle bakers. And just so you don't forget that you're in Boston, the shop also offers stoneware bean pots in seven sizes. Open Monday through Friday 9:00 A.M. to 8:00 P.M., Saturday 9:00 A.M. to 6:00 P.M. Call (617) 523–4039. Most casual strollers are completely fooled by the windows (and the name) of **Dairy Fresh Candies** at 57 Salem Street. They see the local and imported chocolates and miss the extraordinary selection of spices, sauces, specialty cooking oils, and vinegars. Where else in Boston will you find one-ounce tins of saffron at prices that don't break the bank? Open Monday through Saturday 9:00 A.M. to 7:00 P.M., Sunday 11:00 A.M. to 6:00 P.M. Call (617) 742–2639.

Click and Clack Wine and Dine

Tom and Ray Magliozi of National Public Radio's *Car Talk* (alias "Click and Clack, the Tappet Brothers") are down-to-earth guys who like their Italian food traditional. For North End dining, they're partial to two places with great Italian-American atmosphere and classic kitchens: **Ristorante Bella Vista** at 285 Hanover Street, where they recommend the spicy lobster fra diavolo, and **Piccola Venezia** at 263 Hanover Street, where they're partial to the fried calamari.

Bella Vista is open daily noon to 11:30 P.M. Moderate. Call (617) 367–4999. Piccola Venezia is open daily 11:00 A.M. to 10:00 P.M. Moderate. Call (617) 523–3888. If you're a real traditionalist, try Bella Vista's tripe and Piccola Venezia's scungilli (sea conch) salad.

The small stretch of Richmond Street between the North End's main drag of Hanover Street and historic North Square is one of the richest lodes to mine in the neighborhood. **Salumeria Italiana** at 151 Richmond Street has been a neighborhood fixture for generations, a single stop where you can find sausages, cheeses, olive oils, and specialized canned goods for an Italian feast. It's open Monday through Saturday 8:00 A.M. to 6:00 P.M., closed Sunday. Call (617) 523–8743. Just a few doors down is the fashion side of Italian-American culture. **High Gear Jewelry** at 139 Richmond Street specializes in very-high-quality costume jewelry to achieve a penthouse look at a basement price. It's open Tuesday through Friday 10:00 A.M. to 6:00 P.M., Saturday 10:00 A.M. to 9:00 P.M., Sunday 11:00 A.M. to 7:00 P.M. Call (617) 523–5804.

If you really want to make a distinctive fashion statement, don't leave the North End without stopping at **christina defalco** at 383 Hanover Street. This shop features the deliberately mod-retro clothing of the local designer of the same name. To complement her silk-screened T-shirts, pleated miniskirts, vinyl raincoats, and stretch pants, Defalco also carries unique bags and jewelry from other designers in the United States and abroad. The shop is open Monday through Friday 11:00 A.M. to 7:00 P.M., Saturday 11:00 A.M. to 6:00 P.M., and Sunday noon to 5:00 P.M. Call (617) 523–8870.

East Boston

These days, East Boston is reinventing itself, but that's nothing new. Originally a patch of islands on the northeast side of Boston Harbor, East Boston was farmland in the Colonial era and one of the great shipbuilding centers in the mid-nineteenth century. Donald McKay's shipyards on Border Street perfected the "Yankee clipper," the swiftest cargo ship ever to carry sail into the wind.

But by the first decades of the twentieth century, East Boston was better known as a port of entry (or sometimes of quarantine) for immigrants from Europe.

East Boston was transformed in the mid-twentieth century, when much of the waterfront was seized by eminent domain to make way for Logan International Airport. Today long stretches of the waterfront are windswept, weedy lots where rotting pilings are the only reminders of the neighborhood's distinguished maritime past. Characteristically, Bostonians who come to East Boston only to catch a plane love to lament what was lost. Most significantly, Logan obliterated Wood Island Park, a Frederick Law Olmsted landscape, and fragmented the neighborhood. Eastie today consists of a group of squares at the end of the harbor tunnels and west of the airport, and a strip leading up the highlands of Orient Heights. Massport, Logan's parent agency, continues to control most of East Boston's waterfront property, and the roar of jet engines is a constant reminder of Logan's busy flight schedule.

downunder

When the subway tunnel to East Boston opened in 1904, it was the first underwater transit tunnel in the country.

earlyflight

Logan International Airport opened in 1923.

East Boston's ethnicity has continued to shift over the years. In the mid-twentieth century, it was a largely Italian-American neighborhood with some traces of earlier Irish immigration. In the early twenty-first century, it is primarily a Latin American neighborhood of Salvadorans, Guatemalans, Colombians, and Brazilians, with a significant Southeast Asian community as well. Spanish vies with English as the language of everyday commerce, and many signs are posted in Spanish and Portuguese, then in English almost as an afterthought. But the days of East Boston's identity as a frayed-cuff, working-class neighborhood may be numbered. A sizable contingent of visual artists has begun settling in the neighborhood, attracted by great views, inexpensive rents, and cavernous warehouse and loft spaces. Where artists go in Boston, condo developers usually follow.

Although Bostonians on "the other side" (as folks in Eastie

forbiddenfruit

When Logan International Airport was expanded in the 1950s, it absorbed Governor's Island, where John Winthrop— or possibly his predecessor Roger Conant— planted the country's first pear and apple trees in 1623.

refer to the rest of Boston) often consider East Boston beyond the pale, the neighborhood is tightly and conveniently linked to the rest of the city by the MBTA Blue Line, with stops in Maverick Square, Logan Airport, Wood Island, and Orient Heights. Free two-hour parking is available on the streets in East Boston, but the T is the simplest way to begin exploring the neighborhood.

To drink in the Latin flavor of East Boston, you need only walk around **Maverick Square,** the neighborhood's first stop on the Blue Line. Probably the first thing you will notice is the heady aroma of roasting chicken and the limed-corn smell of hot tortillas as they singe on a grill. No one with a taste for Mexican and Central American cooking need go hungry here. For a quick snack, stop in at **Rosticería Cancún** at 37 Maverick Square. The eatery is about the size of a large phone booth and although there is a counter along one wall, most patrons stop in for hand-held food (giant burritos, especially) that they can eat on the run. Breakfast Salvadoran style—eggs, beans, and plantain—is served all day. Open daily 8:00 A.M. to 7:00 P.M. Call (617) 567–5808. Inexpensive.

Directly across Maverick Square, **La Sultana** at 40 Maverick Square (617–568–9999) is a classic bakery-restaurant of the type found throughout Latin America. Breads and pastries (many filled with tropical fruit pastes) line the cases, but over the course of the day, La Sultana turns its ovens and stoves over to more solid fare. Around lunchtime, La Sultana fills up with patrons feasting on the barbecued chicken plates. You can almost tell if the diners hail from the Caribbean islands or from Central or South America by whether they choose rice or potatoes, respectively, to accompany their chicken, salad, and beans. La Sultana is open Monday through Friday 6:00 A.M. to 8:00 P.M., Saturday and Sunday 7:00 A.M. to 9:00 P.M.

Fans of Latin music of almost any stripe must walk a short distance out of the square to pop into **El Palacio de la Musica** at 24 Chelsea Street. El Palacio carries CDs and tapes of everything from Puerto Rican salsa to Uruguayan cowboy music, from Mexican polka bands to Brazilian jazz. One of the specialties is Colombian music. You'll need some patience to browse through the dense stacks of recordings in this small shop, but owner Augusto Arango is happy to help. East Boston has many music stores, but we know of no other that can match El Palacio's selection from non-U.S. recording studios. The store is open Monday through Saturday 10:00 A.M. to 9:00 P.M., Sunday 1:00 to 8:00 P.M. Call (617) 569–2427.

The almost seamless transition from Italian neighborhood to Latin-American neighborhood is nicely reflected in the quirky **Saints & Angels** store at 167 Maverick Street. As the name suggests, the shop sells Roman Catholic ceramic religious figures, including a rather dramatic version of Archangel

Michael vanquishing a snakelike Satan at the gates of Heaven. You can buy prepainted figures or purchase white bisque versions and your own paints to decorate them. The store also sells ceramics supplies and teaches classes. Saints & Angels is open Tuesday through Saturday 10:00 A.M. to 4:30 P.M., closed Sunday and Monday. Call (617) 567–4077.

At the end of the block, **DeAngelis Bakery** at 175 Maverick Street has been baking bread in its brick oven since 1917. This neighborhood institution produces old-fashioned, soft-crust Italian breads, along with cookies and cannoli. Open Monday through Friday 9:00 A.M. to 5:00 P.M., Saturday 9:00 A.M. to 3:00 P.M. Call (617) 567–9383.

If you continue down Maverick Street to Cabot Street and turn right, you will approach the East Boston waterfront at the showpiece, six-and-a-half-acre **Piers Park,** which was officially dedicated in 1996. The broad recreational landscape with playgrounds, picnic tables, and ornamental plantings was a long time coming. It materialized as a form of reparation to the citizens of East Boston for the seizure of Wood Island Park. The most prominent feature of the park is a 600-foot pier paved with brick and lined with pavilions whose sailing-ship and wave shapes evoke the neighborhood's maritime past. There's really no better place in Boston for a front-row seat on the harbor and the Boston skyline. The park's tiered amphitheater hosts concerts in the summer and becomes an ice-skating rink in the winter.

The **Piers Park Sailing Center** predates the park by a year. This private, nonprofit group promotes Boston Harbor sailing with classes and a fleet of 23-foot sloops. The programs are geared primarily to residents (adult season passes start at $625), but if you'd like a taste of sailing and a chance to take a quick spin in the harbor, consider a three-hour introductory sailing class. Also check with the center for open house dates, when you can get a free sailboat ride. The sailing center is at 95 Marginal Street. Call (617) 561–6677 or visit www.piersparksailing.org.

If you walk back up Cabot Street and turn left on Sumner Street, you'll go past the Lewis Mall, with views down to the water. On the corner of Maverick Square, **Taquería Cancún** at 192 Sumner Street has four booths and seven tables in a cheerful yellow dining room with television sets tuned to Spanish telenovelas. If you arrive in time for breakfast, try the chicken tamales or cheese pupusas. Later in the day, if you are really hungry, go for the "Montanero," a combination plate of Colombian specialties including

first sign of green

The Boston Celtics won their first NBA championship in 1957.

grilled steak, pork rind, egg, fried sweet plantain, rice, beans, and salad. You can wash it down with a banana or strawberry milkshake. Open daily 8:00 A.M. to 11:00 P.M. Call (617) 567–4449. Inexpensive.

Lo Presti Park occupies the point at the end of Sumner Street. Located directly across the harbor from Long Wharf, this green space has fabulous views of the main Boston waterfront and the piers of the North End as well. If you want to feel truly privileged, wait your turn for one of the two tennis courts. Winner gets to serve facing the harbor.

Despite the popularity of baseball in the East Boston parks (influenced, no doubt, by the Latin stars of the Red Sox), the *Brazilian Soccer House* at 110 Meridian Street represents the sport with which most folks in Eastie identify. Non-players might find it unbelievable that a store could be devoted entirely to soccer, but this shop appears to carry every brand and style of soccer shoe, soccer ball, pads, and even jerseys and shorts. It's open Monday through Saturday 9:00 A.M. to 8:00 P.M., closed Sunday. Call (617) 569–1164.

The authentic northern Italian fare (baked sweet red peppers stuffed with beans, spinach, and cheese, for example) is a good enough reason to stop at *Caffè Italia* at 150 Meridian Street during mealtimes. Between meals, they make an excellent thimble of espresso. But the best time to come by is on Friday and Saturday nights, when a variety of musicians take the floor in the Piano Bar from 9:00 P.M. to 1:15 A.M. Caffè Italia is open Sunday through Thursday 8:00 A.M. to 1:00 A.M., Friday and Saturday 8:00 A.M. to 2:00 A.M.

Flush with Success

Deer Island, at the end of the Winthrop peninsula a short distance from East Boston, has a long history of warehousing what Boston doesn't want. During King Philip's War in the 1600s, the colonists penned up the friendly Native American tribes in the New World's first concentration camp. And Deer Island served as a quarantine station for sick immigrants for more than half a century before World War I. Today the "island" (now a peninsula) is home to a state-of-the-art, $3.8 billion sewage treatment plant. Each day the 212-acre plant treats 450 million gallons of waste that arrives in 11-foot-diameter pipes from the homes of 2.5 million people in Boston and surrounding communities, dumping the disinfected material 9½ miles offshore in Massachusetts Bay. The spotless and odorless facility is an engineering marvel. Each week it produces more than 3.5 million gallons of digested sludge that is turned into fertilizer, most of it sold to Florida citrus growers. The methane created from sludge digestion heats the entire treatment plant. Five miles of walking trails circle the facility, with elevated observation spots and granite benches. Ironically, it's a park without public rest rooms. Tours of the treatment facility are sometimes offered. Call (617) 539–4248 for information.

There are dozens of little ethnic markets and corner stores in East Boston, but for Central and South American specialty foods, we like *Andina Market* at 357 Meridian Street. Miguel and Ana Andrade stock the usual necessities of a neighborhood store, but if you look closely, you'll find the specialty forms of corn flour favored in different parts of Latin America as well as little plastic bags of herbs and spices—*yerba buena,* for example, and *canela,* the splintery New World version of cinnamon. Andina also carries several forms and brands of "table" chocolate for making hot chocolate and other traditional drinks.

Not all of East Boston is concentrated in Maverick, Central, and Day Squares. If you hop on the T and ride outbound to the Orient Heights stop, you can walk to three attractions beyond the dense commercial part of the city. Sandy, well-groomed *Constitution Beach* is a swimming strand only somewhat diminished by the roar of jets taking off and landing. (The jets seem more interesting and dramatic if you don't live in East Boston.) Along with the swimming beach—complete with lifeguards in the summer—Constitution also has basketball, tennis, and handball courts. The bathhouse and other facilities are open Monday through Friday 11:00 A.M. to 7:00 P.M., Saturday and Sunday 10:00 A.M. to 6:00 P.M.

Steeply uphill from the T stop, the *Don Orione Madonna Queen National Shrine* at 111 Orient Avenue occupies a balcony-like overlook that shows the symmetrical beauty of Logan Airport in the foreground with the harbor and the downtown skyline behind. The 35-foot statue of the Virgin Mary that dominates the overlook replicates a statue in Rome sculpted by Italian Jewish sculptor Arrigo Minerbi as thanks for helping him escape the Nazis. The 1954 shrine stands opposite a charitable home for the elderly, fulfilling the principle of the Don Orione Fathers that beside every work of charity, they would build a work of faith. The shrine is open daily 8:30 A.M. to 7:00 P.M. Call (617) 569–2100.

The last surviving Colonial-era salt marsh on Boston Harbor can also be found within walking distance of the Orient Heights T stop. The 350-acre *Belle Isle Marsh* reservation, operated by the Metropolitan District Commission, is a rare successful example of environmental reclamation. In the 1600s the area was used as a sheep-and-cattle pasture and the marsh was harvested for salt hay. Today, it is reverting to its wild state with one important difference: a boardwalk that provides public access. It is one of the top birding spots in the Boston area—not just for terns, egrets, herons, and other aquatic and wading birds, but also for many different raptors, including peregrine falcons, sharp-shinned and red-tailed hawks, kestrels, and snowy owls, which feed on the muskrats and mice that abound in the marshland. The Friends of Belle Isle Marsh, a local environmental group, often presents interpretive programs at the marsh. Call (617) 727–5350 or visit www.friendsofbelleislemarsh.org.

Places to Stay in Charlestown, North End, and East Boston

Boston's Bed & Breakfast Afloat,
Lewis Wharf, North End;
(781) 545–2845.
From May through October, let the waves of Boston Harbor rock you to sleep aboard the 40-foot *Golden Slipper* at the edge of the North End. The private stateroom has a double bed and you'll have a full galley kitchen, with breakfast arriving in a basket in the morning. Moderate.

Harborside Hyatt Conference Center & Hotel,
101 Harborside
Drive, East Boston;
(617) 568–1234 or
(800) 233–1234.
Of all the hotels in and around Logan Airport in East Boston, the Harborside Hyatt gets the nod for its ocean liner architecture and great views across the har-

bor from half the rooms. It's also next to the airport water shuttle dock. Moderate to expensive.

Inn at Crystal Cove,
600 Shirley Street,
Winthrop;
(617) 846–9217 or
(877) 966–8447;
www.inncrystalcove.com.
This beach house inn looks straight across Boston Harbor at the downtown towers from Winthrop, next to Eastie. (Take the Blue Line to Orient Heights, then the Winthrop bus.) Some rooms include private balcony, kitchenette, and harbor views. Four of the thirty rooms share baths. Pet-friendly. Inexpensive.

Shawmut Inn,
280 Friend Street,
North End;
(617) 720–5544 or
(800) 350–7784;
www.shawmutinn.com.
This former office building near North Station and the FleetCenter offers reasonably priced and roomy lodgings for short- or long-term stays. All rooms include microwave and refrigerator. Moderate.

Places to Eat in Charlestown, North End, and East Boston

Caffè Italia,
150 Meridian Street,
East Boston;
(617) 569–1800.
See page 70 for full description.

Daily Catch,
323 Hanover Street,
North End;
(617) 523–8560.
Also known as "The Calamari Cafe," this Neapolitan fish house goes heavy on the garlic and is best known for its fried squid. No reservations, so be prepared to wait. Open Sunday through Thursday 11:30 A.M. to 11:00 P.M., Friday and Saturday 11:00 A.M. to 11:30 P.M. Moderate.

Figs,
67 Main Street,
Charlestown;
(617) 242–2229.
The first of super-chef

AUTHORS' FAVORITES IN CHARLESTOWN, NORTH END, AND EAST BOSTON

Charles River Dam and Locks

Warren Tavern

Bocce courts at Puopolo Park

Dairy Fresh Candies

Salumeria Italiana

El Palacio de la Musica

Piers Park

AUTHORS' FAVORITE PLACES TO EAT IN CHARLESTOWN, NORTH END, AND EAST BOSTON

Figs	Taquería Cancún
Maurizio's	Santarpio Pizza
Pizzeria Regina	Topacio Restaurant

Todd English's restaurants, Figs is a great place to dine on hearty baked pastas and thin-crust pizzas without quite the scene of its sister restaurant, Olives. Open Monday through Saturday 5:30 to 10:00 P.M., Sunday 4:30 to 9:00 P.M. Moderate.

Ida's,
3 Mechanic Street, North End; (617) 523–0015. The ultra-hospitable Bruno family make you feel at home in this tiny restaurant down an alley off Hanover Street. Every dinner comes with spaghetti and salad, and almost every prepara- tion can be assembled with chicken, veal, or eggplant. Open Thursday through Saturday 5:00 to 10:00 P.M. Inexpensive.

Ironside,
25 Park Street, Charlestown; (617) 242–1384. Restaurant staff from around the city often wind down at the Ironside bar when they get off work. But during mealtime this surprisingly stylish pub can turn out excellent pork chops or baked salmon. Meals served weekdays 11:30 A.M. to 10:00 P.M., Saturday

and Sunday 5:00 to 10:00 P.M. Moderate.

La Sultana,
40 Maverick Square, East Boston; (617) 568–9999. See page 68 for full description.

Maurizio's,
364 Hanover Street, North End; (617) 367–1123. The Sardinian-born chef and owner, Maurizio Lodo, is a genius with fish, and works powerful magic with pork and poultry as well. Try to get a table near the kitchen to watch Lodo work, and order from the daily specials to benefit from his latest inspiration. Open for lunch Wednesday through Saturday noon to 3:00 P.M., dinner Tuesday through Saturday 5:00 to 10:00 P.M., Sunday 2:00 to 10:00 P.M., closed Monday. Moderate.

Olives,
10 City Square, Charlestown; (617) 242–1999. The top reason people go to Charlestown is to see Old Ironsides. The next best reason is to eat at Olives, the flagship of celebrity chef Todd English and one of the

largest, loudest, and hearti- est serious restaurants in Boston. Get there early; the line usually starts forming an hour before opening and reservations are accepted only for large groups. Open Monday through Friday 5:30 to 10:15 P.M., Saturday 5:00 to 10:15 P.M., closed Sunday. Expensive.

Paolo's Trattoria,
251 Main Street, Charlestown; (617) 242–7229. The wood-fired brick oven drives the best cooking at Paolo's, which specializes in simpler food than most Boston trattorias and then proceeds to execute it per- fectly. Open Monday through Wednesday 5:00 to 9:30 P.M., Thursday through Saturday 5:00 to 10:30 P.M., closed Sunday. Inexpensive to Moderate.

Piccola Venezia,
263 Hanover Street, North End; (617) 523–3888. See page 66 for full description.

Pizzeria Regina,
11½ Thacher Street, North End; (617) 227–0765. See page 62 for full description.

Rino's Place,
258 Saratoga Street,
East Boston;
(617) 567–7412.
East Boston artists make Rino's one of their favorite hangouts—partly because the homemade pasta and eggplant parmigiana are so good, and partly because the food is so reasonably priced. Open Monday 4:00 to 9:00 P.M., Tuesday through Thursday 11:00 A.M. to 10:00 P.M., Friday 11:00 A.M. to 11:00 P.M., Saturday 4:00 to 11:00 P.M. Inexpensive.

Ristorante Bella Vista,
285 Hanover Street,
North End;
(617) 367–4999.
See page 66 for full description.

Rostería Cancún,
39 Maverick Square,
East Boston;
(617) 567–5808.
See page 68 for full description.

Saigon Hut,
305 Meridian Street,
East Boston;
(617) 567–1944.
Saigon Hut is more than just another *pho* place, though the spicy crab soup will warm both body and soul. If you're unfamiliar with Vietnamese cuisine, the shrimp-and-shredded-cabbage salad with fried garlic should open your culinary frontiers. Open daily 11:30 A.M. to 9:30 P.M. Inexpensive.

Santarpio Pizza,
113 Chelsea Street,
East Boston;
(617) 567–9871.
Neither the fight posters nor the Gerber baby-food-jar salt and pepper shakers have changed here in generations. Outstanding barbecued sausage and lamb skewers are grilled over wood charcoal, while thin-crust, garlic-infused pizza comes from the brick oven. No gimmicks, no pretensions—just great pizza and barbecue in a classic neighborhood bar. Open daily noon to 1:00 A.M. Inexpensive.

Taquería Cancún,
65 Maverick Square,
East Boston;
(617) 567–4449.
See page 69 for full description.

Topacio Restaurant,
120 Meridian Street,
East Boston;
(617) 567–9523.
Savvy food lovers from around Boston make the pilgrimage to Topacio for the exquisite Salvadoran version of *sopa de mariscos*—a Latin American version of bouillabaisse that's full of calamari, shrimp, scallops, and clams in the shells. It's served with a lobster tail and claws draped over the side of the bowl. It's accompanied by a stack of thick, homemade tortillas. Open daily 11:00 A.M. to 11:00 P.M. Inexpensive.

Warren Tavern,
2 Pleasant Street,
Charlestown;
(617) 241–8142.
See page 59 for full description.

South End and Roxbury

Online mapping sources consider the South End and Roxbury indistinguishable from one another, yet they have a very different history, geography, and demographics. Both are principally residential and both are in the throes of galloping gentrification, but the South End, with its proximity to Back Bay and downtown, got something of a head start. Roxbury, on the other hand, is just beginning to rise on the tide of prosperity that has lifted the "boats" of other Boston neighborhoods.

Both communities lie west of downtown Boston, to which they are connected via the long thoroughfare of Washington Street, once known as Boston Neck. The isthmus bridged the waters between Boston Harbor and the Charles River swamps to connect Boston on the Shawmut peninsula to Roxbury on the mainland. The marshes surrounding the neck were filled in between 1834 and 1870, creating the land that became the South End.

Roxbury began as sprawling farmland, but developed in the nineteenth century into Boston's first suburb, where tanneries, machine shops, and factories employed Irish and Eastern European immigrants who moved into the area. The South End began as a luxury development akin to Back Bay but slipped into a vast stretch of immigrant tenements following the Panic of

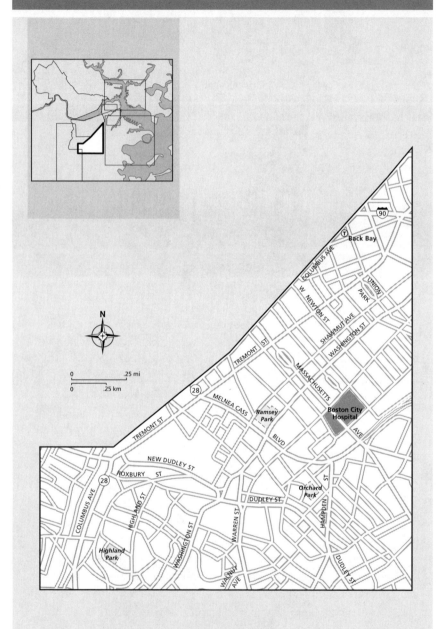

1873 and the subsequent depression that wiped out the neighborhood's real estate speculators. Through most of the twentieth century, the adjoining neighborhoods became predominantly African-American, and Roxbury remains so today.

Distances in this chapter are significant, and a car can come in handy for exploring the entire area. But much of the two neighborhoods can be neatly explored on foot, with long-distance transits via the MBTA bus lines or the T's Orange Line trains. The new Silver Line bus runs along Washington Street from downtown Boston through the South End to Dudley Station in the heart of Roxbury. Although the old maps differ, we have drawn the line between the South End and Roxbury along Melnea Cass Boulevard.

South End

If you're interested in the origins of the South End, consider slogging through *The Rise of Silas Lapham* by William Dean Howells. The book chronicles the brief era during which the neighborhood enjoyed substantial social prestige, before it was overshadowed by Back Bay. You can also find hints of the district's immigrant years in the letters and memoirs of Lebanese-American poet and painter Kahlil Gibran, who grew up in the area between 1895 and 1904 and frequently posed for pioneer art photographer F. Holland Day. And a taste of the African-American neighborhood during the Jazz Age can be garnered from Dorothy West's early fiction. She, too, came of age in the South End. Few physical reminders of Gibran's and West's eras survive, but the fine Victorian town houses on English-style park squares described in *Silas Lapham* have made a dramatic recovery. Architectural historians claim that the South End is the most extensive intact Victorian neighborhood in the country.

The South End is also one of Boston's most racially and culturally integrated neighborhoods. A substantial Puerto Rican enclave occupies the physical center of the district, which is also Boston's largest gay and lesbian community. Like many gentrifying neighborhoods, the South End is home to a substantial

makingway

The first settlement house in Boston, the South End House, opened in 1892 in a remodeled row house on Rollins Street.

contingent of writers, musicians, and artists. It is also one of the great restaurant neighborhoods of the city.

Start your tour of the South End at the Back Bay T station on the Orange Line. Across from Back Bay Station and adjacent to the upscale Copley Place shopping mall, the imposing facade of **Tent City** rises on the corner of Dartmouth Street and Columbus Avenue. This 1989 housing complex—with 25 percent of the units set aside for low-income residents and another 50 percent for moderate-income residents—is named for the 1968 protest in which activists pitched tents on a vacant lot to call attention to the need for affordable housing. Shopping-mall developers created the housing as a "linkage" project, agreeing to build low-income housing in exchange for receiving permits for commercial construction. This interplay of upscale development and social conscience sets something of the tone for the modern South End.

Four long roads extend from downtown Boston to form the residential arteries of the South End: Columbus Avenue, Tremont Street, Shawmut Avenue, and Washington Street. If you walk up Columbus Avenue toward Massachusetts Avenue, at West Newton Street you'll reach one of the finer historic memorials in the neighborhood, **Harriet Tubman Square.** Tubman (1820–1913) was an escaped slave who returned tirelessly to the South to lead others to freedom on the Underground Railroad. A tablet in the square quotes one of her more eloquent speeches: "There are two things I have a right to, and these are death or liberty. One or another I mean to have. No one will take me back alive." Two large-scale statues anchor the ends of the small park. Meta Warrick Fuller's 1913 *Emancipation* dramatizes the human suffering of slavery and the nobility of freedom, while Fern Cunningham's *Step on Board* is a more didactic piece with multiple quotations, a map of the Underground Railroad, and a bas-relief of Tubman leading men and women out of slavery. The original Harriet Tubman House, a settlement house for new Bostonians, was established in the 1890s at 25 Holyoke Street.

greenease

Speaking to the American Social Science Association in 1870, Frederick Law Olmsted cited the social utility of parks, saying, "the beauty of a park should be the other. It should be the beauty of the fields, the meadow, the prairies, of the green pastures, and the still waters. What we want to gain is tranquillity and rest to the mind."

A half block up from Tubman Square, at the corner of Rutland Street, you'll have one of the city's best unobstructed views of a classic Victorian Boston church, **Union United Methodist,** 485 Columbus Avenue, (617) 536–0872. Union United Methodist was built for a Universalist congregation that moved here from School Street in 1872. The structure epitomizes Boston's unique adaptation of Gothic Revival architecture, using the dramatic pudding-stone from Roxbury.

Another church of particular note lies farther out Columbus Avenue, across Massachusetts Avenue: **Columbus Avenue A.M.E. Zion Church,** 600 Columbus Avenue, (617) 266–2758. The march of ethnic history is writ large on the side of this house of worship, where its most prominent window forms the Star of David. Before it became an African-American church, the building was Adath Israel, a synagogue erected in 1884 by the German-Jewish community then prominent in this part of the South End and Roxbury.

Jazz buffs should consider a pilgrimage to the blocks around the intersection of Columbus and Massachusetts Avenues. The modern **Harriet Tubman House,** part of United South End Settlements, stands at 566 Columbus Avenue

Harriet Tubman Memorial

Workin' on the Railroad

It seems fitting that a heroic-scale statue of **A. Philip Randolph** stands in the lobby of Back Bay Station, which is also an Amtrak station. The civil rights leader and union organizer came to prominence by establishing a trade union for Pullman porters in the 1930s. Randolph's union was one of America's first black labor unions. A prominent spokesman for civil rights in the 1940s and 1950s, Randolph was instrumental in President Harry Truman's order to desegregate the armed forces. He also helped lead the 1963 march on Washington that led to the Civil Rights Act of 1964.

on the site of the ***High Hat Club.*** The High Hat was one of the liveliest joints of the Jazz Age, as noted by the murals on the side of the Tubman House. The women's craft collective of the ***South End Community Health Center*** inside the Tubman House sells goods that truly represent the diversity of the community: African-American Raggedy Ann dolls, Guatemalan textiles, Haitian painted wood, and a variety of items featuring ethnic embroidery.

A few buildings toward Back Bay on Massachusetts Avenue is the seemingly unremarkable ***Wally's Cafe,*** its name overwhelmed by a beer sign. Tiny Wally's was founded in 1947 by Joseph "Wally" Walcott, making it Boston's longest consecutively owned black business. Wally's was a stop on the old "Chitlin' Circuit," a tour frequented by Billie Holiday and Errol Garner, and it still jumps with live music starting at 9:00 P.M. Monday through Saturday and at 3:00 P.M. on Sunday. Wally's is at 427 Massachusetts Avenue. Call (617) 424–1408. Just past the A.M.E. Zion Church, you'll find ***Bob the Chef's*** at 604 Columbus Avenue, a "healthy" soul food restaurant and major local jazz hangout with nightly music and a Sunday jazz brunch. Call (617) 536–6204. Both Wally's and Bob the Chef's benefit from their proximity to Berklee College of Music, which has a top-flight program in professional jazz.

No monument marks the spot, but Martin Luther King Jr. lived in the rowhouse apartment building at ***397 Massachusetts Avenue*** when he was studying theology at Boston University. King left Boston in the 1950s but returned in 1965 to lead 10,000 people on a march to Boston Common to protest the racial imbalance in Boston's schools.

If you walk a block down Northampton Street from Bob the Chef's to Tremont Street, you'll encounter one of the most striking of Boston's midnineteenth-century industrial buildings, known colloquially as the ***Piano Factory*** (791 Tremont Street). One of several Boston factories that built pianos, this massive post-and-beam structure was originally constructed in 1853 for the Chickering Piano Company and recycled in 1974 as artists' housing—one of the first such mill conversions in Massachusetts. Although many

Local Knowledge

For a local—and youthful—perspective on the South End, check the schedule of tours offered by **MYTOWN,** which calls itself "the only youth-led historical walking tour in Boston." Well-trained teenaged guides delve into the neighborhood's history while also revealing snapshots of everyday life. A limited number of tours are offered June through September and begin at the Back Bay MBTA station. Call (617) 536–8696 or visit www.mytown.com.

nonartists now share the building, the **Gallery at the Factory** continues to exhibit the work of resident and nonresident artists. The gallery is open Friday 5:00 to 10:00 P.M., Saturday and Sunday noon to 5:00 P.M., and Monday 1:00 to 6:00 P.M. Call (617) 437–9365.

Halfway down Tremont Street, heading back toward downtown, **Villa Victoria** is one of Boston's triumphant stories of community activism blunting the well-intentioned but often socially disastrous effects of "urban renewal." Hundreds of residents, primarily Puerto Ricans, faced displacement in the late 1960s when redevelopment came to Parcel 19—the South End blocks bounded by Tremont, West Dedham, and West Newton Streets and by Shawmut Avenue. The residents organized as *Inquilinos Boricuas en Accion* (literally, Puerto Rican Tenants in Action) and worked with the city and the architectural firm of John Sharrat Associates to develop Villa Victoria. This self-contained community features more than 600 affordable housing units, along with playgrounds, a central plaza, and a few shops and social-service offices. The architecture borrows from the Puerto Rican vernacular, and if you pop in to have a look at the murals, remember that this is private property.

Boston's Longest Park

The longest single park in Boston is **Southwest Corridor Park,** linking the South End with Forest Hills in West Roxbury. When this nineteenth-century railroad corridor was designated in the 1960s as the route for a twelve-lane "inner belt" highway, community protests stopped the highway in its tracks. Planners rethought the area, building instead the T's Orange Line and this 5-mile-long corridor park at a cost of $750 million. On its in-town end, the park divides the South End from Back Bay, link-ing the cul-de-sacs of South End residential streets with a series of green spaces and a broad path for walking, bicycle riding, jogging, and blading. Once the park crosses Massachusetts Avenue, it becomes a true recreational corridor—with playgrounds, tennis courts, basketball courts, and community gardens—for more than 4 miles through Roxbury and Jamaica Plain to the Forest Hills T station.

Celebrate!

The third weekend in July and the third weekend in September offer the opportunity to celebrate two different aspects of South End culture. The **Annual Festival Betances** in July at Villa Victoria features Puerto Rican music, dancing, food, arts and crafts, and sports activities. Call (617) 927–1707 for information. During **September Open Studios,** more than 200 artists invite the public into their work spaces. The largest concentrations of studios are at the Boston Center for the Arts and along the 500 block of Harrison Avenue. Call (617) 267–8862 for information.

The community's *Jorge Hernandez Cultural Center* at 85 West Newton Street frequently hosts Hispanic arts and cultural events. The former church structure has a striking mythic Puerto Rican mural above the front entrance. Call (617) 927–0061. The center features "El Bembe" Latin dancing on Friday nights, with salsa and merengue classes from 9:15 to 10:00 P.M., then dancing until 1:30 A.M. Call (617) 927–1707 or visit www.salsaboston.com.

We like to think of the intersection of Tremont Street with Clarendon Street and Union Park as the entertainment center of the South End, for these corners are dotted by cafes and restaurants and sprinkled with performance spaces and galleries. The studios and practice rooms of the Boston Ballet are just around the corner on Clarendon Street, and the *Boston Center for the Arts (BCA)* takes up the better part of the block between Clarendon and Berkeley Streets. The most intriguing part of the complex is the *Cyclorama* building at 539 Tremont Street. The twentieth-century facade hardly hints at the vast steel-trussed dome inside, constructed in 1884 to house a 400-foot-by-50-foot painting-in-the-round of the Battle of Gettysburg. (The painting is now at Gettysburg Battlefield Historic Park in Pennsylvania.) Over the years, the Cyclorama functioned as an auto parts plant (the spark plug was invented here), a boxing ring (featuring famed bare-knuckler John L. Sullivan, among others), and a wholesale flower market. The vast space is often used for art exhibitions, antiques shows, and live theater. In addition to the Cyclorama space, the BCA's smaller theaters present some of the city's most innovative work by independent theatrical troupes.

The BCA's *Mills Gallery* is also known for its avant-garde exhibitions and installations. The gallery shares the Tremont Estates Building at the corner of Tremont and Clarendon Streets with more than fifty artists' studios and the internationally acclaimed Hamersley's Bistro. Built in the 1860s for an organ company, the building later served as the factory for the "Velvet Grip," the original garter for silk stockings. The Mills Gallery is open Wednesday, Thursday, and Sunday noon to 5:00 P.M., Friday and Saturday noon to 10:00 P.M. Call (617) 426–8835 for the gallery, (617) 426–5000 for the BCA.

Flush with Art

If you have a chance to attend an event at the Boston Center for the Arts' Cyclorama, be sure to go powder your nose. The *award-winning rest rooms* were designed by South End architects Sheila Kennedy and J. Frano Violich. The 1993 project was designed "to heighten the public's awareness of how plumbing connects us all."

To get a feel for what the South End was like in its heyday, cross Tremont Street and walk through *Union Park.* The first square completed in the neighborhood (1857–1859), Union Park was intended as a template for further development, but, to us, nothing quite matches it. Brick Victorian row houses surround a small park with fountains, graceful trees, and that greatest luxury of all in a crowded city, thick green grass. If you have your car, don't even think of trying to park here. Resident-only parking is rigorously enforced.

The artistic and domestic side of the South End finds full-blown expression at *Aunt Sadie's* at 18 Union Park Street (617–357–7117). The owners of Aunt Sadie's make hand-dipped tapers and scented candles, which they sell in galleries and museums around the country. In addition, they carry some unusual handbags and housewares. Aunt Sadie's is open Monday to Thursday 10:00 A.M. to 6:00 P.M., Friday and Saturday 10:00 A.M. to 7:00 P.M., Sunday 11:00 A.M. to 5:00 P.M.

One block in from Tremont, make a left on *Shawmut Avenue,* the least explored of the South End's arteries. Two of our favorite places to shop for food stand side by side in the block between Hanson and Bradford Streets: *Syrian Grocery Importing Company* at 270 Shawmut Avenue and *South End Formaggio* at 268 Shawmut Avenue. Between them, they epitomize the old and new South End.

Syrian Grocery is a survivor from the days when the South End had a large Middle Eastern population—from roughly the 1880s until World War II. Old-fashioned wooden bins and jars of exotic herbs and spices kindle our appetites

Remembering Ben

Benjamin Franklin did not forget his home town in his will—he left Boston the funds to found an institute of practical learning. The *Franklin Institute,* at the corner of Berkeley and Appleton Streets, opened in 1908 and is dedicated to teaching the fundamentals of applied engineering. Among its later supporters was Andrew Carnegie. The institute is now affiliated with Boston University.

every time we walk in. Surely there are other places in Boston to purchase grape leaves, ground sumack, or *za'atar,* but Syrian Grocery gives them a provenance that even the most well meaning chain grocer cannot. It's the only place we've ever found that sells not only Paula Wolfert's books that explain how to make airy, ethereal couscous from scratch, but also the graduated sieves necessary for "rolling your own." Syrian Grocery is open Tuesday through Saturday 11:30 A.M. to 6:00 P.M. Call (617) 426–1458.

South End Formaggio, on the other hand, is a modern marvel of refined taste, specializing in more than 300 cheeses from Europe and the United States. It seems fitting that the man behind the store and its sister operation in Cambridge, Ihsan Gurdal, is also an immigrant, in this case from Turkey. Gurdal, who has become one of America's leading experts on cheese, built his own cellar in 1996 to age his cheeses before offering them for sale. Don't come looking for standard Vermont cheddar or Monterey Jack. Gurdal is more likely to stock a farmstead cheese from a little town in Tuscany, or certain French cheeses so rare that they're hard to get even in Paris. Belying the preciousness you'd expect of such refined taste, Formaggio is a lively little spot that also sells prepared foods to go. In fact, the place is jammed at lunchtime with people ordering grilled sandwiches (say, sliced roast pork with mango salsa) and salads. South End Formaggio is open Monday through Friday 9:00 A.M. to 8:00 P.M., Saturday 9:00 A.M. to 7:00 P.M., Sunday 11:00 A.M. to 5:00 P.M. Call (617) 350–6996.

Adding more multicultural flavor to the street, ***Qingping Gallery Teahouse*** at 231 Shawmut Avenue is a crossroads of old and new, East and West. Gallery owner Wu Xianxin, a Beijing activist, was arrested as a young student during the 1989 Tiananmen Square demonstrations and spent three

The Artistic Fringe

As the South End becomes ever more desirable real estate, establishments devoted to non-mainstream artistic expression move to the edges. Case in point: 450 Harrison Avenue/31-47 Thayer Street, a massive former industrial building now full of artists and interesting galleries and shops. No fewer than five galleries are found here. The **Bernard Toale Gallery** (617–482–2477; www.bernardtoalegallery.com), the **Clifford-Smith Gallery** (617–695–0255), and the **Genovese-Sullivan Gallery** (617–426–9738) anchor the complex. Relative newcomers on the artistic frontier are the **Allston Skirt Gallery** (617–482–3652) and **O'H&T** (617–423–1677). At the same time, stop by **Bobby from Boston** (617–423–9299) for vintage 1950s clothing and memorabilia or prowl through the architectural salvage treasures of **Restoration Resources** (617–542–3033). Most establishments are open Tuesday through Saturday 10:30 A.M. to 5:30 P.M.

years in jail. Later he owned a restaurant and an art gallery in Beijing before coming to the United States in 1996. Qingping (pronounced "Ching-ping") features a striking gallery of avant-garde Chinese art on the second level and the low-key teahouse on the ground floor. Tea is pricey—up to $7.00 a pot—but

palace for the dispossessed

The Pine Street Inn, the city's largest shelter for the homeless, is located on Harrison Avenue in a Victorian building based on the Palazzo Vecchio in Florence, Italy.

you're buying more than rare, gourmet teas. You're purchasing some moments of serenity. Qingping Gallery Teahouse is open daily from noon to midnight. Call (617) 482–9988.

If you return to Union Park and continue south until it crosses Washington Street, you'll be greeted by the massive expanse of the *Cathedral of the Holy Cross,* the largest Roman Catholic church in Massachusetts (roughly the size of England's Westminster Abbey). Completed in 1875, Holy Cross was erected (on the site of the municipal gallows) to serve the largely Irish congregants who had settled in the marshland shantytowns of this part of the South End and adjacent lower Roxbury. At the time, Fort Point Channel stretched behind the cathedral up to what is now Massachusetts Avenue. Manufacturers set up shop along the channel to take advantage of easy shipping, and their workers lived in cheap housing nearby. Both the industrial sites and the shanty housing have long since vanished, and the congregation today is substantially Hispanic. Although the cathedral was constructed, in no small part, to serve the poor, it presents a majestic figure of Roxbury puddingstone elegantly trimmed with brick and Quincy granite. The cavernous interior echoes with the deep tones of a powerful Hook & Hastings organ, ranked among the city's finest liturgical instruments. Even the windows bespeak old-world elegance, as many contain rare stained glass from Munich. The cathedral seats 3,500 in the pews and will accommodate 7,000 people standing for major events and feast days. It is open daily from 9:00 A.M. (after Mass) until 3:00 P.M. No tours.

Roxbury

Founded, like Boston, in 1630, Roxbury had resources that Boston lacked—ample farmland, good timber, and Roxbury puddingstone, an excellent and easily quarried building stone. As Boston grew into a densely populated trade port, Roxbury flourished as Boston's countryside, where large farms supplied the city and in-town gentlemen built their country retreats. Only with the growth of Boston's suburbs in the mid-nineteenth century did Roxbury finally come entirely under Boston's sway, voting for annexation in 1868.

For practical purposes, Roxbury can be divided into two areas: the industrial lowlands adjacent to Boston Neck that were created when the marshes were filled in during the early nineteenth century, and the original highlands of glacial drumlins that rise abruptly from Dudley Street west to Grove Hall and Franklin Park. The original Roxbury Center was at Eliot Square, a little north of Dudley Square at the juncture of the highlands and lowlands. The area now known as Dudley Square developed as the city's first commercial center, and so it remains. The main streets of the square—Washington, Eustis, Warren, and Dudley—all date from the first decade of settlement, and Dudley Square makes a perfect place to begin exploring. It's certainly easy to get to— buses from all over Boston and the western and southern suburbs feed into Dudley Station, the city's busiest MBTA stop. Perhaps the easiest is the no. 1 bus, which runs along Massachusetts Avenue from Cambridge through Back Bay and the South End to Dudley. In fact, Dudley was the terminus of Boston's first "mass transit"—horse-drawn omnibuses that ran from downtown out Washington Street in the 1820s.

Since the 1940s, Dudley Square has been the commercial hub of Boston's African-American community—and more recently of its community of black immigrants from Africa and the Caribbean. Before you do anything else, walk around **_Dudley Station._** Originally built as the western terminus of the Boston Elevated Railway that ran from Boston out to Roxbury, the older part of the station resembles the Beaux Arts railway stations of Europe. Given that he studied at the École des Beaux-Arts in Paris, that was probably the intent of architect Alexander Wadsworth Longfellow, nephew of poet Henry Wadsworth Longfellow and member of H. H. Richardson's architectural firm. When the El was dismantled, Dudley became a bus hub and additional platforms were added in Longfellow's style. Pushcart vendors sell everything from tropical fruits to black-history books and West African carvings, street preachers offer salvation over portable P.A. systems, and hundreds of people mill around—a true cross section of the Roxbury community.

Downhill from Dudley Station, the **_John Eliot Burying Ground_** is the oldest remaining slice of original Roxbury. The cemetery at the corner of Washington and Eustis Streets was consecrated by the English colonists in 1630 and continued to function as an active burial ground until the middle of the nineteenth century. The man for whom it is named, John Eliot, was known as "the apostle to the Indians." In the seventeenth century he translated the New Testament into Algonkian and converted many of the Native Americans in Massachusetts to Christianity. Eliot struggled against the governing body of

Massachusetts Bay Colony for more humane treatment of the Native American population, and he was credited by some with nearly averting King Philip's War, in which the Native Americans of New England were decimated.

Just a block up from the burial ground, the **Hamill Gallery of African Art** at 2164 Washington Street can almost serve as a museum, so comprehensive is the gallery's collection of art and artifacts from traditional sub-Saharan African cultures. Featured exhibitions change six times a year, but Tim Hamill always has a broad selection of works on display, including divination objects, helmet masks, batik textiles, exquisite beadwork, and all sorts of decorative, utilitarian, and ceremonial carved objects. The main entrance is at the rear. The gallery is open Wednesday through Saturday noon to 6:00 P.M. Call (617) 442–8204.

If you walk uphill from the Hamill Gallery and take the left fork, you'll be on Warren Street, where it's worth checking out **A Nubian Notion Annex** at 41 Warren Street. The original Nubian Notion, next door in the former Hotel Dartmouth, serves as a neighborhood convenience store, and the gifts, clothing, jewelry, and other items have moved into the annex. The family-run operation has been a central part of Dudley Square's identity since the late 1940s. Need a Malcom X cap or poster, or a collection of his speeches? How about some West African carvings? Bolts of batik fabric? Handmade jewelry? Nubian Notion is the long-standing connection to the mother continent and to contemporary threads of African-American culture. The shop also sells and rents videos and maintains a casual table for flyers that functions as a community bulletin board. Call (617) 442–2622.

The convenience-store side of Nubian Notion holds down the ground level of the **Hotel Dartmouth,** an 1871 Second Empire–style structure with its marble facade hidden beneath layers of peeling paint. The development agency Nuestra Comunidad purchased the building in the summer of 2001 with the aim of restoring it and constructing apartments and artists' lofts on the upper levels. The same agency produced the handsome rehabilitation of Paladio Hall across the street.

Some striking pockets of colonial and Victorian Roxbury lie within walking distance of Dudley Square. At the corner of Warren and Dudley Streets, turn right and walk about a quarter-mile, looking uphill for the spire of First Church Roxbury, which marks **John Eliot Square** (not to be confused with John Eliot Burying Ground). You'll also see a few small signs pointing to Roxbury Heritage State Park.

At the top of the hill, make your first stop the **Dillaway-Thomas House** at 183 Roxbury Street. Built as a parsonage between 1750 and 1754, the house had an unparalleled view of Boston Neck, the slender peninsula that connected Boston to the mainland. For this reason, it became the headquarters for

General John Thomas of the Continental Army during the Siege of Boston. A telescope in the outdoor garden demonstrates that even today one can keep a close eye on downtown. The house became the private home of the Dillaway family in 1835 and underwent several architectural transformations before the city purchased it in 1927. It stood vacant for decades, suffering near-destruction in a 1979 fire. In 1992 the Department of Environmental Management took over the structure and repaired and enlarged it as the centerpiece of the Roxbury Heritage State Park. Among the massive oaks and maples on the grounds is the only healthy, mature American chestnut tree we have ever seen in New England. The gardens are also planted with Roxbury Russet apple trees, a locally developed and highly prized cider apple. Call (617) 445–3399 for tour hours, usually Wednesday through Friday.

Eliot Square was a great place to keep an eye on the British Army, but Roxbury was virtually destroyed during the Revolution. One of the major reconstruction efforts was the **First Church Roxbury,** built in 1804 on the site of the original 1632 meetinghouse. This handsome white church, so typical of those throughout New England, is currently being restored under the auspices of the Unitarian-Universalist Urban Ministry.

If you follow Highland Street up from the pointed end (north side) of Eliot Square, you'll walk through a neighborhood of primarily Victorian houses and row houses with the sounds of saws and hammers ringing out their open windows. This part of Roxbury is scrambling to bring handsome old homes back to elegance. Across from 120 Highland Street, **Rockledge,** the home of William Lloyd Garrison, stands behind a high black iron fence. Editor of the *Liberator* and one of America's fiercest abolitionists, Garrison built this imposing home of Roxbury puddingstone in the 1840s. In 1864, a year after President Lincoln declared Emancipation, Garrison and his wife retired to Rockledge, where Garrison died in 1879. The mansion is now St. Mary's Convent.

Sweet Stone

Roxbury puddingstone is an unusual conglomerate stone found only in the Roxbury highlands west of Boston. Glacial in origin, it was formed by the compacting of glacial rubble with the clays found offshore in Boston Harbor. The practical Puritan founders of Boston used the stone extensively as a building material. Architect H. H. Richardson popularized puddingstone again in the nineteenth century as appropriately rustic for his neo-medieval designs. Frederick Law Olmsted also employed Roxbury puddingstone extensively in his landscape designs, finding its rough textures evocative of the natural world.

Near the crest of Highland Street, make a right onto Fort Street and you'll arrive at Roxbury's crowning glory, **Highland Park.** The Continental Army fortress built here during the Siege of Boston was torn down in 1869 to make way for the water standpipe that still towers atop the hill.

tophonors

Frederick Law Olmsted considered his design for Franklin Park one of his three finest achievements, ranking it with Manhattan's Central Park and Brooklyn's Prospect Park.

In 1888 the land was designated Highland Park and in 1895 Frederick Law Olmsted designed the landscape, placing the borders and supporting walls of puddingstone.

Other major sites in Roxbury are best toured by car. From Dudley Square, follow Warren Street west and make a right onto Walnut Avenue. In just a few blocks, Walnut crosses Dale Street, where you can see the **Malcolm X House** at 72 Dale Street, just two houses from the intersection. This was the home of teacher Ella Little-Collins, Malcolm Little's sister, when Malcolm X was still known as "Detroit Red" and worked as a soda jerk, a Parker House busboy, and a burglar. Ella encouraged her brother to study law and theology during his stay in Norfolk Prison, where he embraced the Nation of Islam; he founded Mosque 11 in Dorchester after his release. (Louis Farrakhan succeeded him as minister.) Ella's son lives in the house now, and there is periodic talk of turning it into a museum.

Watch the signs carefully, as Walnut Avenue zigs and zags before you reach the **Museum of the National Center of Afro-American Artists (NCAAA)** at 300 Walnut Avenue. The Victorian Gothic mansion, Abbotsford, was built in 1872 for industrialist Aaron David Williams in the middle of 150 acres of farmland and orchards. (The Williams apple was almost as famous as the Roxbury Russet.) In 1976 the NCAAA transformed the house into the only New England museum devoted exclusively to African, Caribbean, and African-American art.

Fore!

The eighteen-hole **Franklin Park Golf Course** is the second oldest municipal course in the United States. Thoroughly restored with new turf, wide-open fairways, and a comfortable club house, it's one of the few spots in Boston where visitors can routinely get tee times. The entrance is at 1 Circuit Drive. Residents weekdays $22, weekends $28; non residents weekdays $25, weekends $32; seniors $2 less on weekdays. Call (617) 265–4084.

forthebirds

The most impressive of the permanent exhibits is the burial chamber of the Nubian king Aspelta, ruler of the largest empire on the Nile. Open Tuesday through Sunday 1:00 to 5:00 P.M. Adults $4.00. Call (617) 442–8614.

Continue following Walnut Avenue and make a left onto Washington Street, then another left onto Columbus Avenue (Route 28). You'll soon come to the juncture with Blue Hill Avenue and the entrance to the 527-acre *Franklin Park,* the largest bauble of Frederick Law Olmsted's Emerald Necklace. Olmsted considered Franklin Park one of his greatest masterpieces. What he could not have counted on was that in the twentieth century the surrounding neighborhoods would fall into disrepair and that the city would long decline to maintain the park. As a result, Olmsted's grassy meadows once kept cropped by herds of sheep have been transformed into an urban golf course and many of his trails and walkways have been swallowed by trees and weeds. But there are bright spots from the neglect: Franklin Park serves as a refuge for many forms of wildlife, especially songbirds, and the zoo, which was installed over Olmsted's protests, has grown into a city treasure—if an underappreciated one. The *Franklin Park Zoo* at 1 Franklin Park Road has made great strides toward modernization and now ranks as one of America's leading zoos. Open April through September Monday through Friday 10:00 A.M. to 5:00 P.M., Saturday and Sunday 10:00 A.M. to 6:00 P.M.; October through March daily 10:00 A.M. to 4:00 P.M. Admission: adults $9.50, seniors $8.00, children $5.00. Call (617) 442–2002; www.zoonew england.com.

Also within Franklin Park, the refurbished open-air stage at the *Elma Lewis Theater* honors the neighborhood's longtime arts activist. Children's activities take place during summer days, while theater and music groups sometimes perform in the evenings. Call Boston's Parks and Recreation Department at (617) 635–4505 for information on upcoming events.

Places to Stay in the South End and Roxbury

Best Western Roundhouse Suites,
891 Massachusetts Avenue; (617) 989–1000.
This all-suite hotel in a former railroad roundhouse is convenient to the Southeast Expressway, the South End, and Roxbury. The hotel has a fitness center and serves a complimentary continental breakfast. Moderate.

Chandler Inn,
26 Chandler Street; (617) 482–3450 or (800) 842–3450; fax (617) 542–3428; www.chandlerinn.com.
Tucked into one of the narrow side streets between Tremont and Columbus Avenue off Berkeley Street, the fifty-six-room Chandler Inn offers small but clean and comfortable rooms at—by Boston standards—a budget price. Rates include a light continental breakfast. Inexpensive.

Encore B&B,
116 West Newton Street; (617) 247–3425; www.encorebandb.com.
Co-owners architect Reinhold Mahler and set designer David Miller have infused Encore with dramatic flair. Just off Tremont Street, the South End's main line, the three stylish rooms of this new B&B occupy the top floors of an 1860 Victorian brick town house. Each room has a private bath with shower, a queen-size bed, cable TV with DVD player, and direct-dial phone. The bright breakfast nook is adorned with Miller's striking collection of masks from around the world. Inexpensive to moderate.

Places to Eat in the South End and Roxbury

Abubacar Seafood Restaurant,
2360 Washington Street; (617) 427–0003.
The name could fool you, as curried chicken and curried goat are among the best choices at this small Jamaican restaurant right at Dudley Station. No pork products—this is a Halel restaurant. Cafeteria-style offerings vary daily. Open for all meals Monday through Saturday 6:00 A.M. to 9:00 P.M., Sunday 9:00 A.M. to 6:00 P.M. Inexpensive.

Bob the Chef's,
604 Columbus Avenue; (617) 536–6204.
See page 80 for full description.

Caffè Umbra,
1395 Washington Street; (617) 867–0707.
The name is a play on "shadow," since this smart bistro stands across the street from and literally in the shadow of Holy Cross Cathedral in the neighborhood where South End and Roxbury meet on the Silver Line. Chef Laura Brennan makes her own sausages, which are always a winner with her mustardy potato salad. But Brennan can do subtle flavors as well, pairing steamed mussels with a basil ratatouille or seared sole on a potato–salt cod soufflé. Open for dinner Monday through Thursday

AUTHORS' FAVORITES IN THE SOUTH END AND ROXBURY

Southwest Corridor Park

Boston Center for the Arts

South End Formaggio

Wally's Cafe

Museum of the National Center of Afro-American Artists

Franklin Park Zoo

Dillaway-Thomas House

AUTHORS' FAVORITE PLACES TO EAT IN THE SOUTH END AND ROXBURY

Abubacar Seafood Restaurant	South End Galleria
Hamersley's Bistro	Morse Fish Company
Bob the Chef's	

5:30 to 10:00 P.M., Friday and Saturday 5:30 to 11:00 P.M. Moderate.

Charlie's Sandwich Shoppe,
429 Columbus Avenue; (617) 536–7669.
A classic New England luncheonette these days, Charlie's has been a neighborhood fixture since 1927. Years ago, when many jazz clubs stood on the block and Charlie's kept longer hours, it was one of the few places where musicians could get a bite to eat after the last show. Open Monday through Friday 6:00 A.M. to 2:30 P.M., Saturday 7:30 A.M. to 1:00 P.M., closed Sunday. Inexpensive.

Flour Bakery and Cafe,
1595 Washington Street; (617) 267–4300.
Every gentrifying neighborhood needs a European-style bakery and sandwich shop, and the South End has Flour. Joanne Chang, former pastry chef at some of Boston's top restaurants, makes all the goodies onsite daily. In addition to luscious pastries, Flour is known for its grilled sandwiches. Open Monday through Friday 7:00 A.M. to

7:00 P.M., Saturday 8:00 A.M. to 6:00 P.M., Sunday 9:00 A.M. to 3:00 P.M. Inexpensive.

Hamersley's Bistro,
553 Tremont Street; (617) 423–2700.
Chef Gordon Hamersley's entire French Provincial menu is simultaneously simple and sophisticated, rustic and refined. Desserts are satisfyingly rich. Hamersley's signature lemon-infused roast chicken is our favorite in Boston. Open Monday to Friday 6:00 to 10:00 P.M., Saturday 5:30 to 10:30 P.M., Sunday 5:30 to 9:30 P.M. Expensive.

Icarus,
3 Appleton Street; (617) 426–1790.
South End couples generally consider Icarus the most romantic of the neighborhood restaurants, and chef Chris Douglass never fails to surprise diners with deeply flavorful combinations, such as venison with pomegranates and wild-rice pancakes. Open Monday to Thursday 6:00 to 9:30 P.M., Friday and Saturday 6:00 to 10:30 P.M., Sunday 5:30 to 9:30 P.M. Expensive.

Merengue Restaurant,
156 Blue Hill Avenue; (617) 445–5403.
Near Grove Hall and the entrance to Franklin Park, Merengue serves Caribbean food with an emphasis on freshness and pizzazz. The red snapper seviche, which includes diced green olives in the usual mix of peppers and onion, is especially tangy, and Merengue is one of the few places around that squeezes fresh lemons for every order of lemonade. Open daily for all meals 10:00 A.M. to 10:00 P.M. Inexpensive.

Morse Fish Company,
1401 Washington Street; (617) 262–9375.
Primarily a fresh-fish market, Morse also sells fish dinners and fish sandwiches to eat on the premises or to take out. Open Monday through Thursday and Saturday 11:00 A.M. to 8:00 P.M., Friday 11:00 A.M. to 9:00 P.M., Sunday noon to 7:00 P.M. Inexpensive.

Pho République,
1415 Washington Street; (617) 262–0005.
Urbane and sophisticated Pho République is a little removed from the Tremont Street hubbub, but it's worth

seeking out chef Didi Emmons's sassy versions of French colonial and Vietnamese cuisine, including a wide selection of vegetarian dishes. Open daily for dinner 5:30 P.M. to 1:00 A.M. Inexpensive to moderate.

Rouge,
480 Columbus Avenue;
(617) 867–0600.
Southern decadence (as in New Orleans, y'all) is the theme, and bayou-country tastes are showcased with French and Creole dishes like a boudin sausage that's a true pork hash, or sweet potato and smoked chile pepper soup. The bar scene is as dark and mysterious as a Bourbon Street dive (complete with eight single-barrel bourbons), and the dining room is as bright and cheerful as the legendary Antoine's. Desserts are predictably rich—an individual chocolate Bundt cake with pumpkin ice cream, for example. Open for dinner Monday through Wednesday 5:30 to 10:30 P.M., Thursday through Saturday 5:30 P.M. to 1:00 A.M., Sunday 5:00 to 10:30 P.M. Moderate.

Wally's Cafe,
427 Massachusetts Avenue;
(617) 424–1408.
See page 80 for full description.

South Boston and around South Cove

When you cross the Fort Point Channel on Summer Street, a large sign proclaims that you have entered South Boston. We can think of no other neighborhood so determined to announce its boundaries, yet South Boston is a comparatively recent phenomenon. It didn't even exist until 1804, when Boston annexed the newly filled marshes south of the original city and east of Boston Neck.

South Boston exploded in the nineteenth century. Its residential area at City Point and in the marshlands that once made up South Cove expanded from a population of sixty in 1804 to more than 60,000 by 1880. Most newcomers were Irish immigrants, separated from the central city by a tangle of rail lines and a long expanse of waterfront factories and warehouses. The distance bred an insularity that persists, making South Boston among the more homogeneous and tight-knit neighborhoods in the city.

But those barriers are falling, as the Seaport area south of the Financial District begins to blossom. The factories are gone, and warehouses once laden with leather goods and woolens now bustle with artists, designers, and pioneers of the electronic frontier. This chapter deals with three distinct areas: the Fort Point Channel and Seaport closest to downtown

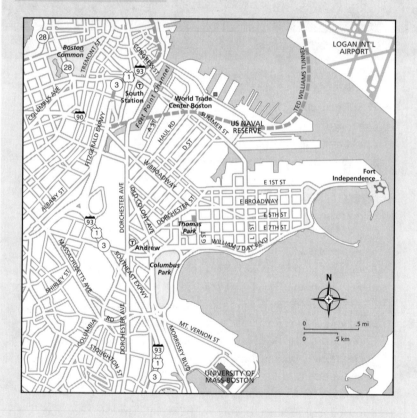

Boston, residential "Southie" with its Irish-American heritage and amazing sandy shoreline, and the densely settled and history-packed corners of Dorchester and Roxbury that once fronted on the tidal waters of South Cove.

bostonshamrocks

South Boston is the third most Irish neighborhood in the United States, lagging behind only two Irish enclaves in New York City.

Fort Point Channel and the Seaport

Boston was a great industrial city a century ago, and towering warehouses and factories were constructed in a restrained but majestic Beaux Arts style on the streets just south of Fort Point Channel. These long courses of brick and stone punctuated by stately rhythms of windows have stood the test of time, largely thanks to a community of visionaries who saw opportunity where others saw disuse and decay.

Former New York mayor Ed Koch once wryly observed that "the role of artists in New York is to make a neighborhood so desirable that artists can't afford to live there anymore." The scenario has been repeated in Boston. In the mid-1970s artists began to establish studios in the low-rent warehouse buildings near Fort Point Channel. Many of these pragmatic pioneers defied zoning restrictions and elected to live in their studios. As the community of artists grew, they banded together to establish permanent live/work spaces. In all, more than 400 artists now live and/or work in the Fort Point district, many of them in two artists' cooperative buildings at *300 Summer Street* and *249 A Street.*

Where artists go, other aficionados of the residential frontier quickly follow. Since the organization of the Fort Point Channel Arts Community in 1980,

Burrowing Through

The most technically challenging segment of Boston's *Big Dig* was the 1,100-foot underground connector linking the Massachusetts Turnpike with the Ted Williams Tunnel. Because there are no steel mills in the area, the roadway, which passes beneath Fort Point Channel, had to be cast in concrete on-site. Nearly half a million cubic yards of earth were excavated to create the casting basin where the tunnel sections were built before they were floated into Fort Point Channel and lowered into place. Each section displaced approximately the same volume as a Navy destroyer.

architects' offices, design studios, dot-com and media companies, and design-oriented furnishings shops have begun to fill the buildings along Summer, Congress, and A Streets. As new restaurants and lounges pop up, Fort Point Channel is emerging as a dynamic bohemian neighborhood. Massive construction projects along the Northern Avenue waterfront—hotels, office buildings, and upscale condos—threaten to overshadow Fort Point (both literally and figuratively), but for the moment this artistic community is blossoming.

To appreciate Fort Point, begin a tour from South Station by walking down Summer Street to cross Fort Point Channel, making the artists' co-op at 300 Summer Street your first stop. It's easy enough to recognize: The building entrance features a dramatic sculpture with a steel canopy, rail, and light sconces created by residents. Even if you miss Open Studios, you can visit the changing exhibitions at the *Fort Point Arts Community Gallery* in the lower level, open Monday through Friday 10:00 A.M. to 3:00 P.M., Saturday noon to 5:00 P.M. Call (617) 423–4299. While you're visiting, you can grab a bite to eat at *Cafe 300,* which nourishes the body the way art nourishes the spirit. Not-so-starving artists come here to nosh on the likes of a roast pear salad with blue cheese and toasted almonds; a sandwich of grilled eggplant, tomato, basil, and mozzarella cheese; or barbecued steak tips with basmati rice—all well under $10. Cafe 300 is open Monday through Friday 8:30 A.M. to 3:30 P.M., Saturday 9:00 A.M. to 2:00 P.M., closed Sunday. Call (617) 426–0695.

On a more theatrical note, *Broadway Costume* at 273 Summer Street rents everything from party and Halloween costumes to specialty duds for theatrical performances. Unless you're willing to go as one of the previous year's hot characters or as a dopey perennial (pirate, fairy princess, etc.), make your Halloween reservations by September. Broadway even outfits costumed weddings. Within the same space, *Jack Stein Make-up Center* specializes in stage, film, and TV makeup as well as wigs and stick-on facial hair. Open Monday through Friday 9:30 A.M. to 6:00 P.M., Saturday 9:30 A.M. to 2:00 P.M. Call (617) 426–3560 for costume rental, (617) 542–7865 for makeup center.

Continue your explorations by descending the metal stairs to A Street, which runs from Fort Point out to residential South Boston. At the foot of the

Fort Point Open Studios

Nearly 20,000 people come to see artists in their lairs during the annual **Fort Point Arts Community Open Studios** on the third weekend of October. More than twenty buildings in the neighborhood house studios, with the largest concentration in the cooperative buildings. Call (617) 423–4299.

stairs, you'll encounter **A Street Deli** at 324 A Street, a neighborhood fixture with cafeteria-style service in the rear. It's one of the great breakfast hangouts in the city, and by early afternoon you'll find construction workers, bleary-eyed artists, Web site coders, and publishing types digging into massive slabs of lasagna and overfilled sandwiches. A Street Deli is open Monday through Friday 4:00 A.M. to 4:00 P.M. Call (617) 338–7571.

One of our favorite designer lighting stores brightens the grimy brick warehouse across the street. **Chimera** at 319 A Street has some of the most ingenious lighting on the market. (We're always fascinated by one lamp that casts a holographic image of a lit bulb, and by the retro-industrial fan lamps from Brazil.) Chimera is open Monday through Friday 9:00 A.M. to 6:00 P.M., Saturday 10:00 A.M. to 3:59 P.M. (The staff admits to jumping the gun to get Saturday night started). Call (617) 542–3233.

After the other large artists' co-op building at 249 A Street, the rest of A Street down to the Broadway T station is resolutely industrial, so turn around and walk under Summer Street to Congress Street, one of Fort Point's focal avenues. Look sharp or you might miss **Lucky's Lounge** at the corner of A and Congress Streets, since the restaurant and lounge doesn't go out of its way to attract new customers, depending instead on a neighborhood clientele who know to head downstairs at the glowing red windows. The junior stock brokers and dot-com execs (at least, those old enough to drink) come in after work, and by late night, this retro Formica-clad room comes into its own as the artists and coders are treated to live music and lounge acts. (Think Frank Sinatra meets Mark Knopfler in the *Twilight Zone*.) "Atomic cocktails" are the favored drinks, but you can also get lunch, dinner, and late-night grub on the order of roast pork, burgers, thin-crust pizzas, and steak tips. Lucky's, at 355 Congress Street, is open Monday through Saturday 11:30 A.M. to 2:00 A.M., with the kitchen closing at 1:30 A.M. Call (617) 357–5825; www.luckyslounge.com.

Fort Point's strong retro streak continues at **Machine Age** at 354 Congress Street. The store specializes in designer furniture circa 1940 to 1975, with an ever-changing stock of rehabbed pieces designed by such gods of Modernism as Charles and Ray Eames, Eero Saarinen, Mies van der Rohe, and Isamu Noguchi. Fortunately for the average buyer's pocketbook, Machine Age also stocks a lot of great Modern Movement furniture without the big names attached. Check the basement for bargain pieces. The store is open Tuesday through Saturday noon to 5:00 P.M. Call (617) 482–0048.

Heading back toward downtown, the **Boston Fire Museum** at 344 Congress Street is a wonderfully authentic little place, staffed largely by former firefighters. This decommissioned fire station contains vintage fire trucks and hoses, photographs from devastating fires of the past, the late Boston Pops

Boston Fire Museum

maestro Arthur Fiedler's collection of fire memorabilia, and a few items (including two chairs) salvaged from the horrific Cocoanut Grove nightclub conflagration of 1942 that forever changed America's fire code. The museum is open Saturday noon to 4:00 P.M. Free admission. Call (617) 482–1344.

Although Fort Point Channel was constructed to give inland Boston access to the sea, the Fort Point Channel neighborhood has been walled off from the harbor by several years of construction and may remain separated by high walls of new development. (Arguments over development plans continue as this book goes to press.) But if you follow Farnsworth Street behind the Children's Museum, a walkway will deliver you to Northern Avenue and the **John Joseph Moakley Federal Court House** on Fan Pier. The courthouse has extremely tight security, but once you surrender your cell phone, camera, and anything else made of metal, you can go upstairs to dine at **Sebastian's Cafe,** the employee and visitor cafeteria with jaw-dropping vistas of Boston Harbor and very reasonable prices. It's open Monday through Friday 7:00 A.M. to 3:30 P.M., closed Saturday and Sunday. Call (617) 261–1911.

On the first Tuesday of every month at 1:00 P.M., volunteers give guided tours of the courthouse. Among the artwork on display are the *Boston Panels,* an art installation of twenty-one colored panels created by Ellsworth Kelly.

Roof with a View

Independence Wharf opened in September 2001, but so far only a few office workers have discovered its hidden fourteenth-floor *outdoor observation deck* that's open to the public. You might want to follow their lead and bring a picnic lunch to eat while you watch planes land at Logan Airport. You can also survey the sweep of skyline from the new John Joseph Moakley Federal Court House on the waterfront to the skyscrapers in Back Bay. On a more practical note, the building also has rest rooms open to the public around the clock. Independence Wharf was built on the site of Griffins Wharf, where tea was dumped overboard from British ships on December 16, 1773. A plaque notes that "To defeat King George's trivial but tyrannical tax of three pence a pound, about ninety citizens of Boston, partly disguised as Indians, boarded the ships, threw the cargoes, three hundred and forty-two chests in all, into the sea, and made the world ring with the patriotic exploit of the Boston Tea Party." The observation deck is open daily from 10:00 A.M. to 5:00 P.M.

You'll also get to see the inside of a courtroom and perhaps even sit in on a court session. Two forms of identification, one with photo, are required for admittance. Call (617) 748–4185.

The waterfront park in the rear of the courthouse offers harbor views almost as good as those from the cafe. It's also a great spot for watching fireworks launched off Long Wharf on First Night.

The distances are long, construction will continue for years to come, and sidewalk crossings are sometimes precarious, so we don't advise walking too far along Northern Avenue. The road extends for the length of the South Boston peninsula past the World Trade Center, home to many small conventions, and Boston Fish Pier, the oldest active fish pier in the country. (The size of the catch here and the resulting prices at the morning fish auction often dictate that

Seeing the Light

America's first lighthouse, *Boston Light,* was erected in 1716 on Little Brewster Island at the mouth of Boston Harbor. It remains the last staffed offshore light in the country. Weekend boat trips from mid-May to mid-October provide a sweeping passage through the harbor and let you visit the Coast Guard's lighthouse museum and climb the seventy-six steps to the top of this venerable beacon. Trips leave from Fan Pier on Saturday and Sunday at 10:00 A.M. and 2:00 P.M. Reservations are required. Admission is $27; seniors, $23; ages six to twelve $17; five and under free. Trips also leave from Fallon State Pier, Kennedy Library and Museum on Thursday and Friday at 10:00 A.M. Admission is $30; seniors, $25; ages six to twelve, $17; five and under free. Call (617) 223– 8666; www.bostonislands.com.

armsofrefuge

In 1847, at the height of the Potato Famine, 25,000 Irish immigrants arrived in Boston.

night's specials at up to a third of Boston's restaurants.) At the eastern end of the peninsula is the Black Falcon Cruise Terminal. Across the Reserved Channel the giant blue cranes of Castle Island Terminal move around the containers carrying much of the $8 billion in goods that move through Boston piers annually.

Southie

While South Boston begins technically at Fort Point Channel, its historic residential district lies farther south and west in a crosshatch of streets dense with wooden triple-decker apartment buildings and the broad *r*-less speech of Southie's overwhelmingly Irish-American population. Developed in the mid-nineteenth century, the eastern end of South Boston, City Point, was originally a Yankee refuge from the tight quarters of Beacon Hill. But the Irish famine quickly changed that, and by the outbreak of the Civil War, virtually all of South Boston housed immigrants from the Old Sod. Those with a little money (not all Irish who fled in the diaspora were poor) took over City Point, while the working class crowded together in the tighter streets west of the point on filled marshland that had surrounded South Cove—a neighborhood once known as Little Galway or the Lower End.

A century and a half later, Southie remains a tight-knit, conservative community where shamrocks often replace apostrophes in store names. But that doesn't mean that people won't greet you on the street or strike up a conversation if you pause to rest on a bench along the beachside walking paths.

Local Suds

Harpoon Brewery at 306 Northern Avenue is South Boston's own microbrewer and the largest brewery currently operating in Massachusetts. It makes a highly regarded India Pale Ale (I.P.A.) as well as several seasonal brews. Buy the sixty-four-ounce "growler" bottle and have it filled with the draft of your choice for a taste of pre-Prohibition days when Boston was awash with breweries. Established in 1986, Harpoon is open Tuesday through Friday 11:00 A.M. to 6:00 P.M., Saturday 11:00 A.M. to 5:00 P.M. with complimentary tours and tastings Tuesday through Thursday at 3:00 P.M., Friday and Saturday at 1:00 and 3:00 P.M. Call (617) 574–9551; www.harpoonbrewery.com.

Bartenders look you in the eye and smile when they ask what you'll be drinking. Views of Boston Harbor are unparalleled, and sandy beaches provide surprisingly good swimming a short ride from downtown.

southie with a beat

Bono of the Irish rock band U-2 credits Boston with the group's first popular and critical success in the United States.

If you're exploring Southie from Fort Point Channel or the Seaport, take the no. 3 or 7 bus to City Point and walk east on East 1st Street toward Marine Park. Alternately, take the T to the Broadway stop on the Red Line and walk the length of Broadway (about 2 miles) or ride the no. 9 bus to Marine Park. You might want to mix walking with the bus ride. West Broadway is Southie's primary business and restaurant district, where new Irish immigrants have transformed a number of once-tired watering holes into stylish pubs with the same kind of contemporary dining you'd find in Dublin or downtown Belfast. Residential East Broadway, especially around Independence Square, is lined with late-nineteenth-century town houses, many of them recently refurbished to sell for half a million dollars or more.

The great bowl of calm water that greets you at the east end of Broadway is **Pleasure Bay,** enclosed on the northeast by Castle Island and encircled by a mile-long causeway. Follow William J. Day Boulevard counterclockwise around Pleasure Bay to reach **Fort Independence Park** on the small hillock of Castle Island, a peninsular knob joined to the mainland by fill in 1891. Southie locals (and Southie-born suburbanites who come to visit) like to soak up the sun at the tables outside **Sullivan's** as they enjoy some fried clams, a hot dog, or perhaps a soft-serve ice cream cone. The snack bar is open March through October daily from 8:45 A.M. until dark. Call (617) 268–5685. If you're driving to South Boston, there's a large, free parking lot in front of Sullivan's at Fort Independence Park.

Recreational fishermen flock to the **Steel Pier,** behind Sullivan's and to the left. The pier juts out at the edge of the navigational channel, enabling anglers to plop bait down in the middle of striped bass and bluefish runs during the warm weather and to catch the occasional flounder during the colder months. A tall granite obelisk at the entrance to the pier honors Donald McKay, the Nova Scotia–born shipbuilder who made Boston clipper ships the pride of the waves in the 1850s. Directly across the harbor, a Logan International Airport runway covers the site of McKay's boat yard.

Castle Island has been fortified continuously since 1634, and the base of the current **Fort Independence** was erected in 1779 under orders from General George Washington, partly to ensure that an enemy could never again occupy Boston. The fort has never seen action, although its substantial batteries were

thebritishreturn

The royal yacht Britannia docked at the Black Falcon Terminal in July 1976, when Queen Elizabeth of the United Kingdom paid a bicentennial visit to the United States.

credited with discouraging British naval attacks during the War of 1812. The fort was manned through the Civil War, when it served as a prisoner-of-war camp. According to local lore, the winner of a duel here in 1817 was walled up in one of the dungeons by friends of the deceased, and, indeed, a skeleton was found behind a wall during a 1905 renovation. An impressionable young private who served at the fort in the 1820s, one Edgar Allan Poe, based one of his most famous stories, "A Cask of Amontillado," on the tale. The current Fort Independence was constructed between 1830 and 1858, then restored in 1989 as a memorial. Volunteers offer tours between Memorial Day and Columbus Day weekends on Saturday and Sunday between noon and 3:30 P.M. Thursday evening sunset tours are also sometimes offered at 7:00 P.M. during June, July, and August, and volunteers report a number of marriage proposals. On the fourth weekend in October, the fort makes an appropriately spooky venue for a Halloween party. Donation requested. For information, call (617) 268–3874 or (617) 268–5744.

Southie residents have taken their constitutionals on the Pleasure Bay causeway since it was constructed in 1886, and on a particularly hot day in 1888, an enterprising newspaper reporter counted 44,000 strollers. Fewer people avail themselves of the cool breezes of the causeway today, but it is still one of the easiest places to spot high-end imported baby carriages, for which South Boston is one of the country's leading markets. You'll also encounter some of Southie's dog owners taking Fido for a stroll—10 percent of the city's licensed dogs reside in South Boston.

Vistas along the causeway are stunning. To the west you can see the glass-and-steel towers of the Financial District and Back Bay. To the north you might spy the smokestack of a cruise ship at Black Falcon Terminal or watch the blue cranes of the shipping terminal shuttle back and forth along the pier. The control tower of Logan International Airport is clearly visible, and planes come in low over the causeway in a thundering, exhilarating rush.

You can swim in Pleasure Bay, but better sandy beaches await you south and west along Day Boulevard. As you follow the sidewalk from the causeway, you'll pass a string of modest nineteenth-century private "yacht clubs"— really social clubs for boaters who share the anchorage off City Point Beach. The yacht clubs bespeak a certain level of exclusivity, but the ***bathhouses*** that stretch between M and K Streets are a legacy of social reform.

The first bathhouses were erected here in the 1860s to make sure the immigrant populations of South Boston could stay clean. But the current long string of bathhouses—separate sections for boys, men, girls, and women—were constructed during the Depression as mayor James Michael Curley's gift to his constituents. In the early twenty-first century, they were renovated to their original Art Deco glory. Mottos incised above the entrances proclaim their lofty purpose: "Let Health My Nerves and Finer Fibres Brace" above the women's entrance, "Cleanness of Body Is Due Reverence to God" above the men's. The *James Michael Curley Recreational Facility* (which members persist in calling the *L Street Bathhouse*) offers changing rooms, health club facilities, classes, and social activities for members. Alas, day passes are unavailable.

The most famous of the bathhouse users are the "L Street Brownies," a group of hardy souls who have begun the New Year with a dip in the ocean at the L Street Beach annually since 1905. For those who aren't quite that adventuresome, the cleanup of Boston Harbor has rendered South Boston beaches safe for swimming on most summer days. A blue flag on the beach signals clean water; a red flag indicates pollution.

A real piece of Southie-ana awaits you a few blocks up L Street from the beach, where *Woody's L Street Tavern* squats on the northwest corner of the East Eighth Avenue junction. Owner Jackie Woods had the good fortune to buy the tavern two weeks before shooting began for the movie *Good Will Hunting*. This typical Southie bar made frequent cameo appearances in the film as the hangout for the genius Will and his Southie buddies. Bumper stickers behind the bar proclaim stereotypical Southie attitudes: "No Liberals," "Forced Busing—Never!" and "St. Patrick's Day Parade, Keep It Straight." (Organizers of the March 17 festivities went all the way to the U.S. Supreme Court to win the right to ban gay and lesbian groups from the parade on the principle of free speech.) A neon shamrock behind the bar promotes Miller Genuine Draft, but most of the taps gush Harpoon ales. A sign identifies Harpoon as Southie's own, with an arrow pointing north and the words "brewed $\frac{1}{2}$ mile."

Splash!

The grassroots environmental group, Save the Harbor/Save the Bay, holds the annual *Swim for Boston Harbor,* usually on the first Saturday in August at the South Boston beaches. Designed to celebrate the cleanup of the harbor and the restoration of the swimming beaches, the festivities include a 1-mile competitive swim and a beach party with activities for children and adults. Call (617) 451–2860; www.savetheharbor.org.

neverforget

Woody's L Street Tavern remains a classic neighborhood hangout, but the locals are accustomed to visitors. The bartender will gladly pull out the scrapbook of clippings about *Good Will Hunting* and the bar, which includes several pages of visitor comments. When we stopped by for a drink, he made a point of showing us the table where the cast members sat. "That's where she told all them dirty jokes," he said. Then he pulled a plastic Oscar statuette from behind the bar and made us pose at the table while he snapped our photo. What can we say? It's a friendly place. L Street Tavern, at 658A East 8th Street, is open Monday through Saturday 11:00 A.M. to 1:00 A.M., Sunday noon to 1:00 A.M. Call (617) 268–4335.

If you walk uphill 2 blocks and turn left on East 6th Avenue, you'll run straight into Thomas Park at G Street. Atop the green park stands the **Dorchester Heights Monument,** the most far-flung piece of Boston National Historical Park. The 1898 monument marks the heights that American troops fortified with cannon to force the evacuation of the British from Boston in 1776. Although the hill was lowered in the nineteenth century to create more land along the shoreline, the view across the mouth of Boston Harbor is still commanding. Fortunately for General George Washington, the British did not know how little shot and powder the Americans had on hand to use in those cannons, which they had trucked 300 miles across the wilderness from Fort Ticonderoga. "When I was a kid, I used to come up here to look for bullets," a middle-aged Southie man told us one day when we were visiting. The 215-foot marble monument is officially open from late June through Labor Day weekend on Saturday and Sunday from 10:00 A.M. to 4:00 P.M., Wednesday 4:00 to 8:00 P.M. Free admission. Call (617) 242–5642. Be sure to check in advance, as the monument sometimes closes when the park service is short-staffed.

As you descend from the heights back toward the harbor on G Street, you'll pass the infamous **South Boston High School,** site of riots and mayhem over racial integration in the 1970s, before reaching the north end of *Joe Moakley Park* (formerly Columbus Park). Renamed for the beloved congressman from South Boston who died in 2001, the park is a broad stretch of playing fields and picnic areas. At the south end of Moakley Park stands the **James Brendan Connolly Memorial.** This son of Irish immigrants won a gold medal in the triple jump at the first modern Olympics in 1896. Before his winning jump, he was reported to have shouted, "This is for Galway!" Connolly went on to win medals in subsequent Olympic games and wrote more than fifty novels and 200 short stories about the sea.

Across Day Boulevard from Moakley Park is the largest of South Boston's strands, **Carson Beach.** The view from the beach takes in the stunning modern blocks of the John F. Kennedy Library and Museum on Columbia Point and the Neponset River gas storage tank splashed with a vibrantly colored abstract painting designed by artist Corita Kent. If you've been hankering to swim but wondering where to change, the Carson Beach Bath House is open to the general public; it has rest rooms, concessions, and foot showers. To head back to public transportation, walk to the traffic circle on the dogleg of Moakley Park. Preble Street leads quickly to the Andrew T station on the Red Line.

Around South Cove

Early maps of Boston, Roxbury, and Dorchester show a shoreline radically different from today's. Boston jutted out to the north as a two-pronged peninsula, reaching toward Charlestown. It was joined to the mainland by a thin isthmus, the Boston Neck. A narrow body of water, South Cove, separated Boston Neck from the larger east-reaching peninsula of Dorchester Neck. The waters of South Cove penetrated southward along Boston Neck to the present-day site of Andrew Square. Except for the narrow cut of Fort Point Channel, South Cove was filled in during the nineteenth century to create new land for a burgeoning population. This short tour along the cove's former shoreline crisscrosses the Roxbury-Dorchester boundary as it connects isolated pockets of

On Point

The most prominent institution on Columbia Point (also known as Harbor Point) is the Kennedy Library and Museum—an attraction so compelling that this otherwise distant peninsula lies well *on* the beaten track. If you visit, don't miss some of Columbia Point's other sights. The grounds of the **University of Massachusetts at Boston,** a campus of monumental brick buildings, are sprinkled with contemporary sculpture on short-term loan from the artists through the Arts on the Point program. The Massachusetts Archives Building (next to the Kennedy Library) houses the **Commonwealth Museum.** Temporary exhibits highlight aspects of state history or unusual materials from the archives. The state archives are also a deep resource for people researching family history, with materials that range from vital records to passenger lists of ships of immigrants to military records and judicial proceedings. The building is open Monday through Friday 9:00 A.M. to 5:00 P.M., Saturday 9:00 A.M. to 3:00 P.M. Free admission. Call (617) 727–2816; www.state.ma.us/sec/arc.

Yankee and Puritan historic sites surrounded by vibrant, ethnically diverse neighborhoods.

On the new land, **Andrew Square** was named for the governor who raised the famous 54th Regiment of free black soldiers in the Civil War, and is the starting point of this walking loop. You can walk to Andrew Square from South Boston or you can take a bus or subway to the Andrew T station. New immigrants are helping this currently shabby square bounce back from decades of adversity, but there's little to linger over yet. Southampton Street leads west from the square, crossing over South Bay Shopping Center and the Southeast Expressway. The shopping center lies in the heart of the portion of South Bay that was dredged in the 1830s to provide fill to Chinatown to support Boston's first railroad lines.

At Newmarket Square, turn left to follow the railroad track past the huge food warehouses established in the 1960s to replace then-decrepit Quincy Market. Continue down the street to Massachusetts Avenue, where the Victoria Restaurant perches at what was once the low-tide mark of South Cove's southernmost reach. When you cross Massachusetts Avenue, Shirley Street will take you through a residential part of Roxbury that dates from the early nineteenth century, when salt marshes were filled to make way for workers' housing.

Just 4 blocks down Shirley Street, the land suddenly rises on a series of glacial bluffs. On the highest point stands the **Shirley-Eustis House,** which you'll approach from the rear. This striking Georgian home was constructed between 1747 and 1751 by William Shirley, then royal governor of the Massachusetts Bay Colony and later commander-in-chief of all British forces in North America. As governor, Shirley had launched the 1745 British expedition that captured the French fortress at Louisbourg on Cape Breton in Nova Scotia, and he used his spoils of war to construct this bucolic retreat on 33 acres in Roxbury. One of Boston's few National Historic Landmarks that predates 1750, the house served as barracks for American troops during the Siege of Boston. It was also the home of William Eustis, a surgeon who served as James Madison's Secretary of War and then as governor of Massachusetts in the 1820s. Like many old manses, the Shirley-Eustis House fell on hard times in the late nineteenth century. Nonetheless, it benefited from one of the city's earliest preservation efforts, and has been largely restored to circa 1825. Slowly but surely, the association that cares for the house is reestablishing an apple orchard of varieties cultivated by Caroline Langdon Eustis, William's widow.

The original carriage house was demolished long ago, but it has been replaced by the very similar **Ingersoll-Gardner Carriage House,** originally built in 1806 in Brookline and inherited by Jack and Isabella Stewart Gardner (best known for her museum) in the 1840s. It was moved to Roxbury and restoration was completed in 2001. Most Boston carriage houses have been transformed into living spaces, but this building retains most of its original structure and even displays vintage carriages of the late eighteenth and early nineteenth centuries.

rockofages

Among the notables interred at Old Dorchester Burial Ground are William Stoughton, chief justice of the colony's witch trial courts, and minister Richard Mather, who begat a dynasty of Puritan theocrats.

The Shirley-Eustis House, 33 Shirley Street, Roxbury, is open for tours May to early October Thursday through Sunday from noon to 4:00 P.M. Admission is $5.00 for adults, $3.00 for seniors and children under twelve. Call (617) 442–2275; www.shirleyeustis house.org.

Shirley Street ends in less than a block, at Dudley Street, where you should turn left to head toward Uphams Corner. By the 1850s this neighborhood was already flourishing, and in 1857 the Metropolitan Railroad established horse-drawn streetcar lines that ran to Boston. The cars were housed at 504 Dudley Street and the building next door was the horse barn. The line went electric in 1892, and three years later the terminus was relocated about a mile west to Dudley Square. (See "South End and Roxbury" chapter.)

If it's a weekend, consider a detour down East Cottage Street to *Maxwell Flea Market* at number 65. Follow the signs around to the back of the building, which is filled with stalls of all kinds of assorted surplus goods, attic and basement lots, and a wide range of miscellany, most at bargain prices. It's open Saturday and Sunday 8:00 A.M. to 4:00 P.M. Call (617) 929–1072.

Dudley Street becomes an increasingly busy commercial center as you approach *Uphams Corner,* the northern village of the original city of Dorchester, founded in 1630. (Commuter rail trains depart from the Uphams Corner station to downtown Boston every hour for $1.25 or a T token.) At Columbia Square, where Dudley Street meets Columbia Road, you'll encounter the stately grounds of *Old Dorchester Burial Ground,* open daylight hours. The cemetery dates from 1633 and remained in use until the early twentieth century. Many of the old stones are weathered and others are gone, but it's a fascinating place to study the other-worldly iconography of Puritan gravestone engravers.

Just a block from the square, going uphill, the *Strand Theatre* at 543 Columbia Road was built in 1918 as a 1,400-seat luxury movie palace and vaudeville hall. Today it serves as a combination community arts center and professional rental hall presenting concerts, live theater, religious revival meetings, and other events. Although well removed from Boston's Theater District, the Strand has developed a reputation for fostering nonprofit and often avant-garde local performing arts companies, as well as gospel music concerts. For information on upcoming programs, call (617) 282–8000.

If you're a fan of world music, you'll want to detour past the Burial Ground on Stoughton Street (the continuation of Dudley Street across Columbia Square) to *Island Music* at 114 Stoughton Street. You've probably noticed that a large segment of the Uphams Corner population hails from the Caribbean and West Africa. Although Island Music looks unprepossessing, this small publishing and importing company features an amazing selection of tapes and CDs that includes the full range of Cape Verdean music (from traditional to very hot club mixes) as well as Brazilian, African, and Latin dance music. Island Music is open Monday through Saturday 11:00 A.M. to 5:00 P.M. Call (617) 282–0125.

Back at Columbia Square, follow Columbia Road for 2 long blocks to Edward Everett Square, named for the famed orator who served as Abraham Lincoln's three-hour warmup act at Gettysburg. (He also served as governor of Massachusetts.) Just as Columbia Road turns from the square, you'll see a little house that looks like it was plucked from Stratford-on-Avon. This is the *Blake House,* built around 1650 and moved from Allen Plain in Dorchester to 735 Columbia Road by the Dorchester Historical Society in 1895 to prevent its demolition. It is often called "the oldest house in Boston," though how much of the original structure remains is debatable. Nonetheless, it is a landmark in historic preservation, for it was the first building in the region saved for its architectural features. When available, volunteers lead tours of the house on the second and fourth Saturdays of each month from 2:00 to 4:00 P.M. Donation requested. Call (617) 265–7802.

At Everett Square, follow Boston Street northward. It's hard to believe that this densely populated inner-city neighborhood was some of America's most famous *orchard country* in the eighteenth and nineteenth centuries. Many of the streets perpendicular to Boston Street are named for varieties of pears grown on the Clapp estate, including Mt. Vernon, Harvest, Mayhew, Dorset, and Bellflower. Some orchards remained here into the twentieth century.

The original settler of this stretch was Roger Clapp, who received the property as a royal land grant in 1630. At 199 Boston Street, you'll come to the home of one of his most successful descendants, the *Lemuel Clapp House,* behind a thick wall of lilac bushes. This manse, built in 1710 and substantially expanded in 1767, is the showpiece of the Dorchester Historical Society, which has headquarters next door in another Georgian structure, the William Clapp House. Lemuel Clapp was a tanner, a prominent Puritan, and an American patriot who invited Continental troops to camp on his lawn during the Siege of Boston. His son, William, became especially successful in the nineteenth century as a developer of hybridized pears. His pride and joy was Clapp's Favorite, introduced in 1840 and still grown commercially. The rooms of the house display artifacts from Dorchester Historical Society collections, including a table that was part of the wedding furniture of Lemuel Clapp and his second wife, Rebecca Dexter. The Lemuel Clapp House is open for tours on the second and fourth Saturdays of each month from 2:00 to 4:00 P.M. Donation requested. Call (617) 265–7802.

To complete the walking loop, follow Boston Road northward back to Andrew Square.

Places to Stay in South Boston and around South Cove

Boston Harbor Hotel,
Rowes Wharf;
(617) 430–7000 or
(800) 752–7077;
www.bhh.com.
Set on the in-town side of Fort Point Channel, the Boston Harbor Hotel anchors the bustling downtown waterfront. Expensive.

Doubletree Club Boston Bayside,
240 Mount Vernon Street at Bayside C;
(617) 822–3600 or
(800) 695–8284;
www.doubletree.com.
Adjacent to the Bayside Exposition and Conference Center and close to Columbia Point, the suites of this business-oriented hotel feature wired work desks and small conference rooms. Inexpensive to moderate.

Ramada Inn,
800 Morrissey Boulevard;
(617) 287–9100 or
(800) 886–0056;
www.bostonhotel.com.

Value for the dollar increases as you get a little farther from the city. This modern Ramada, a mile south of Columbia Point, is reasonably convenient if you have your own car. Inexpensive.

Seaport Hotel & Conference Center,
One Seaport Lane (off Northern Avenue);
(617) 385–4000 or
(877) 732–7678;
www.seaporthotel.com.
Floating like an ocean liner on the South Boston waterfront, this anchor for the Seaport offers comfort, convenience, and an overhead walkway to the World Trade Center. Moderate to expensive.

AUTHORS' FAVORITES IN SOUTH BOSTON AND AROUND SOUTH COVE

Fort Point Arts Community Gallery

Machine Age

Boston Light

Pleasure Bay Causeway

Woody's L Street Tavern

Shirley-Eustis House

Old Dorchester Burial Ground

Places to Eat in South Boston and around South Cove

A Street Deli,
324 A Street;
(617) 338–7571.
See page 99 for full
description.

Amrheins,
80 West Broadway;
(617) 268–6189.
A classic American restaurant with uncommonly ornate carved wood decor, Amrheins has been Southie's special-occasion restaurant for generations. Be sure to try the house special, lobster pie. Open Monday through Friday 11:00 A.M. to 10:00 P.M., Saturday 11:00 A.M. to 11:00 P.M., Sunday 9:00 A.M. to 9:00 P.M. Moderate.

Barking Crab,
88 Sleeper Street;
(617) 426–2722.
Boston's only fish shack sits right on Fort Point Channel with great views of the Financial District towers. Open Sunday through Wednesday 11:30 A.M. to 9:00 P.M., Thursday through Saturday 11:30 A.M. to 10:30 P.M. Inexpensive to moderate.

Boston Beer Garden,
734 East Broadway;
(617) 269–0990.
A former firehouse turned well-polished Irish pub, Boston Beer Garden serves credible pub grub along the lines of shepherd's pie, buffalo wings, and fish-and-chips. Open daily 11:30 A.M. to 1:00 A.M. Inexpensive.

Cafe 300,
300 Summer Street;
(617) 426–0695.
See page 98 for full
description.

Jimbo's Fish Shanty,
242 Northern Avenue;
(617) 542–5600.
This T-shirt-and-cutoffs alternative to Jimmy's Harborside Restaurant has great deck seating directly on the water and incredibly fresh fish at reasonable prices. Open Monday through Thursday 11:30 A.M. to 9:00 P.M., Friday and Saturday 11:30 A.M. to 10:00 P.M., Sunday noon to 8:00 P.M. Moderate.

Lucky's Lounge,
355 Congress Street;
(617) 357–5825.
See page 99 for full
description.

No-Name Restaurant,
15$\frac{1}{2}$ Fish Pier;
(617) 338–7539.
Bare-bones dining on whatever fish was plentiful that day at the fish auction. Don't miss the fish chowder. Open Monday to Saturday 11:00 A.M. to 10:00 P.M., Sunday 11:30 A.M. to 9:00 P.M. No credit cards. Inexpensive.

The Playwright Bar/Cafe,
658 East Broadway;
(617) 269–2537.
The Playwright has transformed a long-established bar space into a spiffy, upscale Irish pub with dishes like roasted salmon and pasta tossed with calamari and shrimp. Sunday through Wednesday 11:30 A.M. to 10:00 P.M., Thursday through Saturday 11:30 A.M. to midnight. Inexpensive to Moderate.

224 Boston Street,
224 Boston Street;
(617) 265–1217.
It's a sure sign that Dorchester is heading upscale when sophisticated trattorias like 224 start to pop up. Feast on hearty northern Italian fare for half the price of North End dining. Open Sunday through Thursday 5:30 to 10:00 P.M., Friday and Saturday 5:30 to 11:00 P.M. Moderate.

AUTHORS' FAVORITE PLACES TO EAT IN SOUTH BOSTON AND AROUND SOUTH COVE

Cafe 300

Jimbo's Fish Shanty

The Playwright Bar/Cafe

Brookline and Jamaica Plain

Some of the vaguest boundary lines in Greater Boston surround the town of Brookline and the Boston neighborhood of Jamaica Plain, but the residents of these suburbs immediately west and southwest of Back Bay and the Fenway go to great pains to differentiate themselves from their neighbors. If one were to believe in stereotypes, Brookline would be entirely populated by the navel-gazing, upwardly mobile cast members of the former TV drama *thirtysomething* while the good folks of JP (as Jamaica Plain residents call it) would be the cast of the former show *Freaks and Geeks*, more or less grown up. Neither stereotype holds up to scrutiny, of course, but Brookline's dedication to nesting and noshing and JP's insistence on bohemian good times figure in the texture of daily life in each area.

Both Brookline and JP belong to the Boston bedroom complex sometimes called the "streetcar suburbs" because they grew exponentially with the advent of streetcar service in the nineteenth century. Brookline retains excellent public transportation via the C and D branches of the Green Line. Jamaica Plain, on the other hand, lost its E Line trains along the Arborway a generation ago; however, it still has a string of Orange Line stops along the former railbed of the Boston & Providence Railroad.

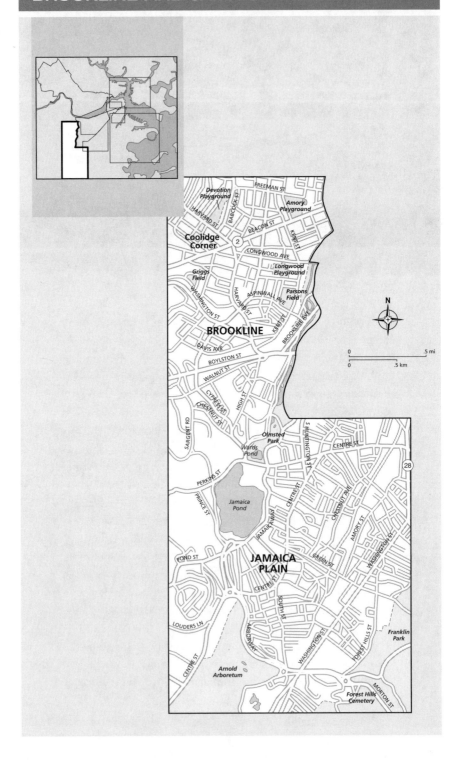

Brookline

Brookline has had its share of famous residents over the years (landscape architect Frederick Law Olmsted, architect Henry Hobson Richardson, and safety razor inventor King Gillette, among others), but few native sons ever achieved such lasting fame as John Fitzgerald Kennedy, born May 29, 1917, in a second-story bedroom at 83 Beals Street. The *John F. Kennedy National Historic Site* (also known locally as the Kennedy Birthplace) receives surprisingly few visitors. Even for Bostonians, the Kennedy Birthplace remains one of those places they mean to get to . . . someday.

cleartitle

The area that is now Brookline was deeded to the Company of Massachusetts Bay by Chief Chicatabut of the Massachusetts tribe in 1643.

The modest frame house of the Kennedy National Historic Site sits on a shady residential street a short walk from Coolidge Corner, one of Brookline's most dynamic village centers. Take the Green Line's C train (Cleveland Circle) to the intersection of Beacon and Harvard Streets, which is Coolidge Corner. Walk 4 blocks north on Harvard Street and turn right onto Beals Street. The house is three-quarters of a block down on the right.

JFK Birthplace

The thirty-fifth president's parents lived in the house from 1914 until 1921, and the Kennedy family repurchased the home in the 1960s to restore it as a memorial to the slain president. Rose Kennedy, John's mother, assembled furnishings, photographs, and mementos to re-create the setting in which JFK was born and spent his early years. Her recorded voice lends an evocative immediacy to the experience.

The John F. Kennedy National Historic Site is open May through October Wednesday through Sunday from 10:00 A.M. to 4:30 P.M. It is closed every Monday and Tuesday throughout the year and is closed from November through April. Guided tours (limited to twelve people per tour) are offered every half hour until 3:00 P.M. Visitors may take a self-guided tour from 3:30 P.M. until closing. Admission is $3.00 for ages seventeen and older. Call (617) 566–7937.

When JFK was four years old, the family moved about a block away to a house on the northeast corner of Abbotsford Street and Naples Road, where he lived until the age of ten. (It is still a private home.) Using a free handout from the National Park Service, you can take a short walking tour through the neighborhood where the future president spent a part of his formative years. A short distance away on Freeman Street is *St. Aidan's Catholic Church,* where the Kennedy children were baptized and the family worshipped. Both JFK and his older brother, Joseph, were altar boys here. An adjacent building, no longer standing, was the site of the Dexter School, a nonsectarian private school that both Kennedy brothers attended. They started school, however, at the *Edward Devotion School* on Harvard Street. In front of the Devotion School at 347 Harvard Street stands the *Edward Devotion House,* an early-eighteenth-century dwelling operated as a house museum by the Brookline Historical Society. The museum is usually open from Memorial Day through October on Tuesday and Thursday from 2:00 to 5:00 P.M. Admission is $5.00. Call (617) 566–5747 to confirm schedule.

This is a good spot from which to launch a walking tour of Coolidge Corner, the self-consciously hip and consumerist center of Brookline, where shops cater to people with a variety of special interests. *New England*

Matters of National Security

In front of the tot lot that adjoins the Devotion School is a small sidewalk plaque noting the importance of 325 Harvard Street to the Allied effort during World War II. The building was the *secret headquarters of the Counter Intelligence Corps* during the early stages of the war. At this facility more than 150 agents were trained in espionage, security, undercover operations, and surveillance.

Comics at 316 Harvard Street (617–566–0115) features all manner of comic books, graphic novels, and underground publications. The most dedicated fans rush the store on Wednesday mornings when the new shipment comes in. The shop is open Monday, Tuesday, and Thursday 11:00 A.M. to 7:00 P.M., Wednesday and Friday 11:00 A.M. to 8:00 P.M., Saturday 10:30 A.M. to 7:00 P.M., and Sunday noon to 6:00 P.M.

Just one door down, on the second floor of the Arcade building at 318 Harvard Street, **Grand Opening!** (617–731–2626; www.grandopening.com) maintains a discreet appearance belied by its wares. This women's erotica boutique tastefully purveys all sorts of appliances, clothing, lotions, and paraphernalia for exploration of sexuality. The glass windows of the store are covered, but photographs show what you will see when you open the door— and it's not the least bit threatening. Open Monday through Wednesday 10:00 A.M. to 7:00 P.M., Thursday through Saturday 10:00 A.M. to 9:00 P.M., and Sunday noon to 6:00 P.M.

For hunger of a more traditional sort, Brookline residents would be hard put to do without the upscale grocer **Zathmary's** at 299 Harvard Street (617–731–8900). Not only does the shop present its produce and meat like so many jewels, it also has a cafe for eat-in and carry-out. Many Brookline professionals with little time to cook stop in after work to pick up sushi, deli salads, lox, hearth-baked pizza, and the like. Zathmary's is open Monday through Friday 10:00 A.M. to 10:00 P.M., Saturday 8:00 A.M. to 10:00 P.M., and Sunday 8:00 A.M. to 8:00 P.M.

The churchlike building at 290 Harvard Street is Brookline's own temple of cinema, the **Coolidge Corner Theatre** (617–734–2500; www.coolidge. org). Constructed as a Universalist church, it made its debut as a cinema on December 30, 1933, with a showing of *Only Yesterday, Saturday's Millions*, and a Disney short. Redecorated to suit its role as an entertainment center, the Coolidge is the only Art Deco theater continuously operating in the Boston area. The theater was threatened with extinction in 1989, but the nonprofit Coolidge Corner Theatre Foundation stepped in to operate the space for art films, independent films, and locally produced films and as a venue for the performing arts.

The intersection of Beacon and Harvard Streets, the epicenter of **Coolidge Corner,** blossomed at the end of the nineteenth century. When electrified streetcars appeared in Boston in 1886, Brookline's Beacon Street was widened into a boulevard, and it began to enjoy elevated streetcar service the following year. The new mobility set off a spurt of development, including the headquarters of an upscale dry-goods dealer, **S. S. Pierce,** in 1898. The ornate building remains a Coolidge Corner landmark.

On an opposing corner, the *Best Cellars* wine store at 1327 Beacon Street (617–232–4100; www.bestcellars.com) is in some regards a modern substitute for S. S. Pierce. The store, part of a small chain that began in New York, specializes in drinkable wines that cost $15 or less per bottle. Their system of categorization emphasizes style ("light," "fresh," "luscious," and other similar adjectives) instead of regional characteristics and grape varietals. The shop hosts tastings every weekday evening from 5:00 to 8:00 P.M. and tastings paired with food Saturday from 2:00 to 4:00 P.M. Best Cellars is open Monday through Thursday 10:00 A.M. to 9:00 P.M., Friday and Saturday 10:00 A.M. to 10:00 P.M., closed Sunday.

Bottle in hand from Best Cellars, traipse up to *Boston Daily Bread* at 1331 Beacon Street (617–277–8810) to buy the other key ingredient for the classic peasant meal of bread and wine. This bakery, which produces some of the metro area's finest sourdoughs, is open Monday through Friday 7:00 A.M. to 8:00 P.M., Saturday 7:00 A.M. to 7:00 P.M., and Sunday 7:00 A.M. to 6:00 P.M.

For folk art, continue along Harvard Street to *Ten Thousand Villages* at number 226 (617–277–7700; www.villages.ca) for a well-curated selection of handicrafts literally from around the globe. The shop (part of a small chain) specializes in "fairly traded" items, in effect guaranteeing that the makers receive a larger-than-customary slice of the purchase price. Open Monday through Thursday and Saturday 10:00 A.M. to 7:00 P.M., Friday 10:00 A.M. to 8:00 P.M., closed Sunday.

Harvard Street continues counting down for another three-quarters of a mile before it reaches its point of origin in Harvard Square, the center of the distinctly ethnic but largely residential *Brookline Village.* It's a fine walk from Coolidge Corner, taking you past such emblems of past waves of immigration as a glatt kosher Chinese restaurant (Shalom Hunan) and a Ukrainian book-shop on the village outskirts. Brookline Village has its own stop on the D (Riverside) branch of the T's Green Line.

If you choose to walk, pause on the final hill rising into the center to have

Crafts Central

The Brookline Arts Center at 82 Monmouth Street has been helping Bostonians with their holiday shopping for almost thirty years. Their **Crafts Showcase** features care-fully selected works by artists and craftspeople from the Boston area and throughout the country. Unlike most such events that take place on one weekend only, the Brookline Arts Center show runs from Thursday through Sunday for three weeks in December, giving ample opportunity to go back for the object that you really regret-ted not purchasing the first time. Call (617) 566–5715 for information.

a look at the often-striking handicrafts and painted objects at **Gateway Crafts Center,** 60 Harvard Street (617–734–1577). The gallery features artists with disabilities. It's open Monday through Friday 11:00 A.M. to 6:00 P.M. and Saturday noon to 5:00 P.M., closed Sunday.

Just up the street, Joe Skokowski maintains the kind of used-book store that makes bibliophiles' hearts beat a little faster. **Albatross Books,** at 45 Harvard Street (617–739–2665), may be small, but the shelves are packed with high-quality older books. The selection is particularly strong in modern literature and poetry, with many first editions and handsomely illustrated small printings. Albatross is open Tuesday through Sunday from noon to 6:00 P.M. (until 8:00 P.M. on Saturday).

At the **Beth Israel Deaconess Friends Thrift Shop** at 25 Harvard Street (617–566–7016), you're as likely to find vintage mah-jongg sets and slightly-the-worse-for-wear fur stoles as sequined cocktail dresses and crock pot slow cookers in yesteryear's fashionable burnt orange or avocado. It's tempting to think that the well-to-do offspring of an earlier generation of immigrants are passing along their belongings to newcomers, but shoppers and donors here come in all ages and ethnicities. The store is nominally open weekdays 10:00 A.M. to 5:00 P.M., but call before heading over. It's staffed by volunteers and actual hours can be erratic.

One of the treasures of Brookline Village is the **Puppet Showplace Theatre** at 32 Station Street (617–731–6400), directly across from the Green Line's Brookline Village stop. Performances for young children are given every Saturday and Sunday at 1:00 and 3:00 P.M. and shows for toddlers are performed on Wednesday and Thursday at 10:30 A.M. Tickets are $8.00.

Several streets (including Harvard, Station, Boylston, and Washington) converge to form "the other" Harvard Square (as opposed to the famed center in Cambridge). This square is ringed with several bars and cafes as well as the "vieux" complex of antiques shops. The mother store of the group is **A Room with a Vieux** at 200 Washington Street (617–277–2700). While other antiques shops in Brookline may be caught in Deco fever, Vieux favors highly ornate French Empire and Louis Napoleon furniture and accessories. It's a particularly good place to browse if you are in the market for a bedroom set. The proprietor scouts out pieces in France every month and the shop usually has about 150 beds and 60 armoires in stock, along with countless nightstands. All the beds can be converted to accommodate queen-size mattresses. Open Monday through Saturday 10:00 A.M. to 6:00 P.M., closed Sunday.

If you want to lounge in style in your new bed, cross the intersection to **Serenade Chocolatier** at 5 Harvard Square (617–739–0795) where you can select a big box of chocolates. This classic candy maker uses Callebaut chocolate from Belgium for "French truffles" dusted in bittersweet cocoa, as well as for truffles flavored with champagne, raspberry, or Grand Marnier. In deference to its name, Serenade sells molded chocolates in the shapes of guitars, pianos, saxophones, violins, and trumpets. The shop is open Monday through Friday 10:00 A.M. to 6:00 P.M. and Saturday 10:00 A.M. to 5:00 P.M. Call (617) 739–0795.

Jamaica Pond and Nearby

Brookline and Jamaica Plain share a long border, obscured in part by the forests, parks, and natural areas along that boundary. Between the two population centers lies *Jamaica Pond.* The glacial knolls, knobs, and drumlins around the 120-acre pond kept the area from development. Until 1848 the pond served as a major source of Boston's water, and it remains a backup reservoir. The spring-fed glacial kettle pond, 65 feet deep in some places, provided such a wonderful natural landscape that when Frederick Law Olmsted sketched out the Emerald Necklace park system, he barely touched Jamaica Pond. His 1882 plan simply graded some banks, planted a few stands of oak and beech trees, and put in pathways.

life is a beach

Prior to the arrival of European settlers, the area around Jamaica Pond was a summer camp for the Wampanoags.

Olmsted's 1.5-mile walking path around the pond continues to fulfill the master's vision as an amenity to encourage residents of the area to take respite in the natural landscape. Joggers, walkers, and strollers from both Brookline and Jamaica Plain throng to use the path, which crosses back and forth between the two areas. The grounds around the Jamaica Pond boathouse serve as a de facto community center from April through November, thanks to the grassroots *Jamaica Pond Project.* (There's a separate bike path partway around the pond, so pedestrians—in theory—don't have to compete with riders.)

Jamaica Pond isn't just a pretty body of water to admire. Anglers find surprisingly diverse species of fish to stalk, ranging from bass and perch in the shallower waters to rainbow, brown, tiger, and brook trout in the pond's colder reaches. (The salmonids are stocked by the state up to four times a year.)

whose woods these are

Arnold Arboretum has a collection of more than 15,000 trees, shrubs, and vines on 265 acres.

Jamaica Pond Boat House

Rowboats are available for rent from late April through most of October (depending on water temperature), and sailboats, including two speedy Laser Boats, can be rented from July through Labor Day weekend. All boat rentals must be reserved in advance and are subject to favorable weather conditions. Hourly rental fees for rowboats are $10.00 for Boston residents, $12.00 for nonresidents, and $5.00 for holders of Massachusetts fishing licenses who use the boats for fishing. Sailboats rent by the hour for $15.00 for Boston residents, $20.00 for nonresidents. Laser Boats are $25.00 per hour or $25.00 for an individual lesson or two-person charter. For information and reservations, call (617) 522–6258.

From the Brookline side of Jamaica Pond, it's just a ten-minute stroll to the home and office of Frederick Law Olmsted, and it only seems proper to pay respects to the architect of so much of Boston's green space. From Jamaicaway, walk up Perkins Street to Cottage Street on the right, then continue a few blocks along Warren Street to the junction of Warren and Dudley Streets. Olmsted dubbed his suburban idyll Fairsted, but the National Park Service calls it the **_Frederick Law Olmsted National Historic Site._** The grounds of Fairsted present an abridged course in Olmsted's design principles, which informed such treasured national landscapes as the grounds of the U.S. Capitol and the White House, New York's Central Park, and, of course, the Boston park system. The site also serves as the National Park Service's center for historic landscape research for the entire national park system. (Frederick Law Olmsted Jr. crafted the now-famous original mission statement of the National Park Service: "To conserve the scenery and the natural and historic objects and the wildlife therein and to provide for the enjoyment of the same in such manner

great oaks from little acorns grow

Arnold Arboretum was the first arboretum in the United States.

and by such means as will leave them unimpaired for the enjoyment of future generations.") The site is at 99 Warren Street. Free guided tours of the house, grounds, and design offices are given Friday through Sunday 10:00 A.M. to 4:30 P.M. Call (617) 566–1689 for information and schedule of free walking tours of the Emerald Necklace.

A close drive from Jamaica Pond, Brookline's *Larz Anderson Park* (617) 739–7518 is a rolling landscape with picnic areas, ball fields, a children's play area, and one of the most striking panoramic views of the Boston skyline from any of the suburbs. This park is the legacy of Isabel and Larz Anderson, who parlayed Isabel's shipping inheritance into a fascinating and productive life in diplomacy and public letters. Come on a clear night from December through February to skate under the stars at the park's *Ice Skating Rink,* open for public skating Friday 7:30 to 9:30 P.M., Saturday noon to 5:00 P.M. and 7:30 to 9:30 P.M., and Sunday noon to 5:00 P.M. Skate rentals are available for $4.50 for all sizes from young children to adults. Adult admission to the rink is $4.00 for residents and $7.00 for nonresidents.

The park is also the home of the *Museum of Transportation,* one of the region's great collections of antique and classic automobiles. The Andersons were early enthusiasts of the motorcar and began buying automobiles nearly as soon as they were available. Their original vehicles constitute the core of the collection, augmented by many restored vehicles that range from early versions of the Model A and Model T Ford to the sumptuously finned behemoths

Man of the People

At 350 The Jamaicaway, practically opposite the Jamaica Pond boathouse, stands a brick Georgian Revival mansion that was the *home of James Michael Curley,* one of Boston's most colorful and corrupt political figures. The interior furnishings are lush—mahogany panels, a crystal chandelier, an Italian marble fireplace, a three-story spiral staircase. Curley lived in comfort while presenting himself as a friend of "the little man." But his command of ward-heeling politics enabled him to get elected mayor, governor of Massachusetts, and member of the U.S. House of Representatives— winning his final election from a jail cell. He served as the thinly veiled model for Frank Skeffington, the protagonist of Edwin O'Connor's *The Last Hurrah.* The City of Boston now owns the house, which is readily identified by the shamrock cutouts in its white shutters. It is open on rare occasions for community events.

of the gas-guzzling 1950s. The Museum of Transportation holds many specialized car rallies throughout the spring, summer, and fall. Open Tuesday through Sunday 10:00 A.M. to 5:00 P.M. Admission is $5.00; $3.00 for seniors, students, and children six and older. Call (617) 522–6547 or visit www.mot.org.

trotlanes

The Arborway, linking Jamaica Pond, the Arnold Arboretum, and Franklin Park, was designed with a carriage road, a saddle path, and a central green pedestrian pathway.

To reach Larz Anderson Park from Jamaica Pond, continue outbound on the Jamaicaway to the traffic circle. One-quarter of the way around the circle is a stoplight at Pond Street. Pond Street changes its name to Newton Street here. The park is on the right, half a mile from the rotary. To reach the park

Rural Rest

At the edge of Jamaica Plain, sandwiched between the Arnold Arboretum and Franklin Park, **Forest Hills Cemetery** was founded in 1848. This pioneer in the Victorian "garden cemetery" movement doesn't get the attention of the slightly older Mount Auburn Cemetery in Cambridge. Nevertheless, it is a stunning place to spend part of a day, appreciating the tranquillity and visiting the resting places of some of the area's political, business, and artistic leaders. Forests Hills' rolling landscape with rocky outcrops contains more than 100,000 graves, including those of Eugene O'Neill and e.e. cummings. Many graves of Boston notables are marked on a map available at the business office at 75 Forest Hills Avenue (617–524–0128). Cummings is buried beneath a flat stone inscribed with his full name, Edward Estlin Cummings, next to a family monument inscribed "Clarke" on the path side, "Cummings" on the back. The cemetery has a magnificent collection of Victorian memorial sculpture as well a growing collection of contemporary work. "Death Stays the Hand of the Artist" near the entrance gates is perhaps the cemetery's masterpiece. The bas-relief is by Daniel Chester French, sculptor of the Lincoln Memorial in Washington, D.C. The cemetery operates programs throughout the spring, summer, and fall. The beautiful and moving Japanese Lantern Festival in July features paper lanterns glowing with votive candles, personalized with messages floating in the twilight on the cemetery's central lake. The cemetery is open daily from 7:00 A.M. to dusk.

To reach the cemetery by public transit, take the Orange Line (or bus no. 39 from Copley Square) to Forest Hills Station, exiting to street level through the Hyde Park exit. Cross Washington Street to Tower Street, and walk up 1 block to the Forest Hills pedestrian gate. By car, follow the Jamaicaway until it becomes the Arborway. Take Route 203 east past the Arnold Arboretum, staying on the overpass above the Forest Hills T station. After the overpass, go through a final rotary and take the first right onto the cemetery driveway.

retiringtype

In 1777 John Hancock moved to Jamaica Plain, after resigning as president of the Congress of the United States.

on public transportation, take the no. 51 bus from the Forest Hills stop on the Orange Line, from the Reservoir stop on the Green Line D branch or from Cleveland Circle on the Green Line C branch. Ask the bus driver to stop at Newton Street. Entrance to the park is a quarter mile up on the left.

"Main" Street, Jamaica Plain

Originally part of the Roxbury Highlands, Jamaica Plain achieved its own community identity by 1683, when it was first mentioned in local records. Like Roxbury (from which it seceded in 1851 with Roslindale and West Roxbury), Jamaica Plain was pastoral for much of its early history. Its orchards hung with Roxbury Russet apples and many varieties of pears, and the verdant countryside made JP an ideal spot for rich Bostonians to build country estates. Among them was Commodore Joshua Loring, a former privateer, veteran of the British Navy, and agent for the British crown. Loring's Georgian manse presided over substantial farm acreage when he erected it in 1760, though the adjacent roads were already developing into a village center.

The home is a little hard to visit today, but the ***Loring-Greenough House*** at 12 South Street is the key to much of Jamaica Plain's history. The Lorings were staunch Loyalists—one son was a British tax collector—and the family

Old Sod and New Spice

It's worth detouring down South Street to visit two landmark ethnic eateries near the Arborway end of Washington Street. Ever since Irish pols began to displace their Yankee counterparts, **Doyle's** at 3484 Washington Street (617–524–2345) has been a must-stop on the vote-getting circuit. Every mayor since Honey Fitz, Rose Kennedy's father, has glad-handed at this 1882 pub. Beer, ale, and Irish whiskey are the favored drinks, and corned beef and cabbage are on the menu every Thursday and on St. Patrick's Day. Otherwise, it's stick-to-your-ribs pub fare. Practically next door at 3492 Washington Street is **Jake's Boss Barbecue** (617–983–3701), where Kenton "Jake" Jacobs displays a mastery of regional seasoning and grilling techniques. All the forms of barbecue are good, but we're partial to the "chopped BBQ" and the "burnt ends" of smoky stewed brisket. Both spots are inexpensive. Doyle's is open daily 9:00 A.M. to midnight. Jake's is open Monday 4:00 to 10:00 P.M.; Tuesday, Wednesday, and Sunday 11:00 A.M. to 10:00 P.M.; Thursday through Saturday 11:00 A.M. to 11:00 P.M.

hightailed it back to London in 1775. Through the Siege of Boston, the house served variously as a commissary, a hospital, and headquarters for American troops. In 1780 it returned to private hands and passed down through four generations of the David Stoddard Greenough family. It was converted to a house

museum in 1926. Because it remained a gentleman's estate throughout most of its history, the rooms of the house reflect different eras from the late eighteenth through the late nineteenth centuries, and the family members who occupied the house were an eccentric and colorful lot. Volunteer guides from the Jamaica Plain Tuesday Club, which owns the building, give often-chatty tours throughout the year, usually on Tuesdays and Saturdays, though the schedule varies with the seasons. Admission is $3.00. Call (617) 524–3158.

You can reach the Loring-Greenough House by walking down Eliot Street from Jamaica Pond, or by taking the no. 39 bus from Back Bay Station or Forest Hills Station to the Civil War Monument, which defines the intersection of Centre and South Streets. If you take a close look at the fence around the monument, you'll find a granite block inscribed "B5," which indicates that this spot is 5 miles from the State House on Beacon Hill. (There's another marker at Hyde Square; that one is marked "B4.")

To get a feel for Jamaica Plain in all its diversity, walk along Centre Street from the Loring-Greenough House all the way to Hyde Square. The first quarter-mile segment is a quintessential concentrate of the "new JP," where body art and Birkenstocks conjoin in the alt-culture mix and small coffee shops and casual restaurants provide a plethora of places to simply hang out. Amid the real estate agents (JP's a hot housing market these days) and other standard community merchants (such as a hardware store), you'll find small emporia of a more unusual

Todo el Mundo

On the Sunday after Labor Day, Jamaica Plain hits the streets between Hyde Square and Jackson Square for the *Jamaica Plain World's Fair.* As with most such celebrations, that means a lineup of arts and craft vendors and food stalls. But in JP, it also means a booty-shaking assortment of spirited music that can range from mambo to salsa to out-and-out, go-to-church gospel music.

sort. For example, **Gadgets** at 763 Centre Street (617–524– 6800) is a tiny store that specializes in peculiar and useful kitchenware. Virtually every cubic inch of space is filled with something—pastry brushes, specialized peelers and zesters, little paper hats to cap the bones on a rack of lamb, and cookie cutters in hitherto unimagined shapes. The store is open Monday, Tuesday, and Saturday 10:00 A.M. to 6:00 P.M., Wednesday 10:00 A.M. to 7:00 P.M., Thursday and Friday 10:00 A.M. to 8:00 P.M., and Sunday noon to 5:00 P.M.

JP is rife with resale shops—Goodwill, church basements, and others— but our favorite of the bunch is **Boomerangs!** at 716 Centre Street (617–524– 5120), where the proceeds benefit the AIDS Action Committee's program to assist people living with HIV/AIDS. The staff at Boomerangs! is committed to moving the merchandise; pricing always aims for the low side on the theory that the charitable work will fare better by selling in volume. We load up on 75-cent paperback books to take on long plane or train rides and leave behind. Open Monday through Saturday 10:30 A.M. to 7:00 P.M., Sunday noon to 6:00 P.M.

The original site of **J. P. Licks Homemade Ice Cream** at 659 Centre Street (617–524–6740) functions as a kind of community center. You can't miss the cow-plastered facade. This purveyor of premium ice cream and frozen yogurt (and their own fresh-roasted coffee) opened in 1981. They also have scones, bagels, croissants, and muffins for those who don't crave ultrarich frozen confections for breakfast. All the food is kosher certified. Open daily 6:00 A.M. to midnight.

El Cubano Verdadero

Among aficionados of casual American dining, the "Cuban sandwich" is the best thing to sweep the United States since the hot dog. A proper Cubano consists of roast pork, ham, cheese, a special marinade/sauce, pickles, and assorted salad vegetables pressed inside a long roll. The restaurant **El Oriental de Cuba,** at 416 Centre Street (617–524–6464), offers Cubanos among their many specialties, but this sit-down family restaurant is a better bet for full meals such as the delicious ropa vieja (Latin pot roast on rice with beans). Open Monday through Saturday 8:00 A.M. to 9:00 P.M., Sunday 8:00 A.M. to 8:00 P.M. For a livelier rendition of the Cubano but a more limited overall menu, try instead **El Miami** at 381 Centre Street (617–522– 4644), the self-proclaimed "King of the Best Cuban Sandwiches." (We concur.) A pair of televisions hangs off the wall over the bar where you place your order, and during the baseball season they'll be humming along with the fastballs of El Duque and Pedro Martínez. It seems like every Dominican or Cuban player who comes into Boston to play for or against the Red Sox has his picture on the wall. Miami is open daily 8:00 A.M. to 11:00 P.M.

If you continue walking down Centre Street, the funky Slacker City begins to morph into Little Santo Domingo as you approach Hyde Square. ***Botanica Anaisa*** (617–522–4565) at 610 Centre Street provides the first hint of what's to come. The

real estate agent

In 1856 Gleason's Pictorial wrote that "Jamaica Plain is a bright pearl in the coronet of rural gems which encircle Boston like a tiara. . . ."

shelves are laden with herbs and tonics from throughout the Caribbean and Latin America. Many of the extravagant labels suggest miraculous cures, or at least assistance with various ills of the flesh. Anaisa also sells a wide variety of Roman Catholic statuary for spiritual help. The shop's hours are Monday through Saturday 10:00 A.M. to 7:00 P.M.

One of JP's hipper outposts is ***Rhythm & Muse*** at 470 Centre Street (617–524–6622), a bookstore and music shop that specializes in local authors and local bands. Slide on the headphones to listen to samplers of some of Boston's most obscure new musical groups, or slip a dollar in change into the poetry vending machine. Of course, you can also buy CDs, tapes, vinyl records (!), chapbooks, magazines, and books. The store is open Tuesday and Wednesday 11:00 A.M. to 7:00 P.M., Thursday through Saturday 11:00 A.M. to 8:00 P.M., Sunday noon to 6:00 P.M.

Stony Brook—Here's Mud in Your Eye

From the 1850s to the 1880s, German immigrants flooded into the section of Jamaica Plain near Roxbury known as Stony Brook, and they brought their thirst with them. At one time Jamaica Plain boasted more than a dozen breweries serving the Greater Boston region. Today there is only one, and it is more a spiritual than a linear descendant of the old-time beer makers killed off by Prohibition.

But, oh, what a brewery! The **Samuel Adams Brewery** of the Boston Beer Company at 30 Germania Street (617–368–5080; www.samadams. com) was a key player in reviving Americans' taste for beer brewed from deeply roasted malts and spicy hops. The brewery offers tours (followed by a tasting) Thursday at 2:00 P.M.; Friday at 2:00 P.M. and 5:30 P.M.; and Saturday at noon, 1:00 P.M., and 2:00 P.M. From May through August, there is an additional tour on Wednesday at 2:00 P.M. A $2.00 donation goes to a local charity.

To reach the brewery by public transportation, take the Orange Line to the Stony Brook station. Above ground, turn left onto Boylston Street, then make your first right onto Amory Street. Take the first left onto Porter Street to the brewery gate. The brewery is at the end of Porter Street on the right.

jp'sfirstbrewer

Samuel Adams moved to Jamaica Plain in 1794.

The pizza joint *Bella Luna* (617–524–6060) and the *Milky Way Lounge and Lanes* (617–524–3740) form a mini dining and entertainment complex at 403–405 Centre Street. Bella Luna's pizzas feature a light, crisp crust with more than forty toppings that range from asparagus and bananas to zucchini and soy "cheese." They also serve dinner entrees such as roasted chicken. The Milky Way is the basement bar, with live music almost every night, except Sundays, when a psychic takes the stage. If you're just too hip for all of that, you can bowl some pins at the Milky Way lanes. Bella Luna is open Sunday through Wednesday 11:30 A.M. to 10:00 P.M., Thursday through Saturday 11:30 A.M. to 11:00 P.M. Milky Way is open daily 6:00 P.M. to 1:00 A.M.

As you begin to approach the plain-vanilla shopping center in the heart of Hyde Square, you'll suddenly stumble into a mother lode of ethnic music in Boston. The *JP Record Shop* at 319-B Centre Street (617–971–0836) specializes in what we think of as Latin Easy Listening. Along with the CDs of sweet-faced singers, they also sell beepers, cell phones, and overseas calling cards, and they make money transfers. The store is open Monday through Saturday 9:00 A.M. to 8:00 P.M. Across the street is the decidedly more colorful *Franklin's CD* at 314 Centre Street (617–522–9745). The Dominican owner Franklin Cabral, himself a musician, is pictured with many Dominican celebrities. Among them is Red Sox pitcher Pedro Martínez, who proclaims the shop his favorite music store. With more than 10,000 titles of Latin music to choose from, it's no wonder. Franklin's CD is open Monday through Thursday 9:30 A.M. to 8:00 P.M., Friday and Saturday 9:30 A.M. to 9:00 P.M., Sunday 11:00 A.M. to 5:00 P.M.

Tucked into the corner of the shopping center at 315 Centre Street is the venerable *Skippy White's* (617–524–4500), a place of pilgrimage for fans of gospel, blues, and R&B music. A large portion of the stock consists of vintage LPs and CD/cassette reissues of music once only available on 78 rpm records. White has an encyclopedic knowledge of gospel and blues and hosts a Saturday-night radio program on UMass Boston's WUMB (91.9 FM). The store is open Monday through Wednesday 10:00 A.M. to 6:00 P.M., Thursday 10:00 A.M. to 8:00 P.M., Friday 10:00 A.M. to 7:00 P.M., and Saturday 10:00 A.M. to 6:00 P.M.

Places to Stay in Brookline and Jamaica Plain

Beacon Townhouse Inn,
1023 Beacon Street,
Brookline;
(617) 232–2422 or
(888) 714–7779.
The sixteen rooms in this lovingly renovated brownstone near the Fenway all feature either king beds or two doubles, plus private bath, refrigerator, and microwave. Rate includes continental breakfast. Inexpensive.

Brookline Manor Inn,
32 Centre Street,
Brookline;
(617) 232–0003 or
(800) 535–5325;
www.brooklinemanorinn
.com.
This Coolidge Corner turn-of-the-twentieth-century lodging has thirty-five nicely appointed rooms. Accommodations range from suites with small kitchens to high-ceilinged rooms with king beds and fireplaces, to smaller rooms with double beds and fire-places. Inexpensive to moderate.

Holiday Inn Brookline,
1200 Beacon Street,
Brookline;
(617) 277–1200;
www.holidayinnbrookline
.com.
The library-style lobby signals that this is one of the Holiday Inns with a touch of grace. Located just outside Coolidge Corner. Moderate.

Longwood Inn,
123 Longwood Avenue,
Brookline;
(617) 566–8615.
This large Victorian house with twenty-two rather simple rooms can be a heck of a bargain—if you can get in. Many of the guests stay for weeks at a time for classes at the nearby medical complex. Rooms have air-conditioning and kitchenettes, and there's free parking and ready access to the Green Line. Inexpensive.

Taylor House Bed and Breakfast,
50 Burroughs Street,
Jamaica Plain;
(617) 983–9334;
www.bbonline.com/ma/
taylorhouse/index.html.
This pond-side 1855 manse opened as a B&B in 1996 and currently has three spacious rooms with private baths at the top of an elegant Victorian staircase. It's less than a block from Jamaica Pond. Inexpensive to Moderate.

Places to Eat in Brookline and Jamaica Plain

Arbor,
711 Centre Street,
Jamaica Plain;
(617) 522–1221.
Chef-owner Douglas Organ has been a hit in JP since he opened in June 2003 with this small (just thirty-eight seats) restaurant with big Mediterranean flavors. Look for surprising combos

AUTHORS' FAVORITES IN BROOKLINE AND JAMAICA PLAIN

John F. Kennedy National Historic Site

Coolidge Corner Theatre

Albatross Books

Jamaica Pond

Fairsted

Franklin CD

Forest Hills Cemetery

AUTHORS' FAVORITE PLACES TO EAT IN BROOKLINE AND JAMAICA PLAIN

El Miami

Zaftig's Delicatessen

Tacos El Charro

Jake's Boss Barbecue

of sweet and salty, like the watermelon-and-feta-cheese salad with arugula, or the thin corn-and-chicken soup flavored with chunks of pancetta and broad shavings of parmigiano cheese. Organ is unafraid to pit big flavors against one another—roasted wild salmon with a generous dollop of salsa verde, for example. Open for dinner Tuesday through Thursday 5:00 to 10:00 P.M., Friday and Saturday 5:00 to 11:00 P.M. Moderate.

Bella Luna,
403–405 Centre Street, Jamaica Plain; (617) 524–6060. See page 128 for full description.

Bukhara Indian Bistro,
701 Centre Street, Jamaica Plain; (617) 522–2195. Indian goes upscale at Bukhara, which offers both northern and southern Indian cuisines. The northern food dominates, though, with rich biryanis (basmati rice, meat, and vegetables baked with spiced yogurt) and an extensive selection of lamb dishes. Open Monday through Thursday 11:30 A.M. to 11:00 P.M.,

Friday 11:30 A.M. to midnight, Saturday noon to midnight, Sunday for brunch from noon to 3:00 P.M. Inexpensive to moderate.

Doyle's,
3484 Washington Street, Jamaica Plain; (617) 524–2345. See page 124 for full description.

El Miami,
381 Centre Street, Jamaica Plain; (617) 522–4644. See page 126 for full description.

El Oriental de Cuba,
416 Centre Street, Jamaica Plain; (617) 524–6464. See page 126 for full description.

Jake's Boss Barbecue,
3492 Washington Street, Jamaica Plain; (617) 983–3701. See page 124 for full description.

J.P. Seafood Cafe,
730 Centre Street, Jamaica Plain; (617) 983–5177. This just might be JP at its multicultural finest: a Korean/Japanese seafood restaurant where everyone comes for the tempura,

sushi boats, and roast fish. There are also many vegetarian dishes. Open for lunch Monday through Saturday 11:30 A.M. to 2:30 P.M., for dinner daily 5:00 to 10:00 P.M. Inexpensive to moderate.

Pho Lemongrass,
239 Harvard Street, Brookline; (617) 731–8600. Hardly just another soup house, Pho Lemongrass serves a wide range of Vietnamese food, attracting not just the thirtysomethings of Coolidge Corner but Brookline's knowledgeable Southeast Asian residents as well. Open Sunday through Thursday 11:00 A.M. to 10:00 P.M., Friday and Saturday 11:00 A.M. to midnight. Inexpensive to Moderate.

Tacos El Charro,
349 Centre Street, Jamaica Plain; (617) 522–2578. Ai-yi-yi-yi! This is the only casual Mexican restaurant we know of in Boston where the owner's mariachi band plays on the weekends. From the Frida Kahlo and Emiliano Zapata murals at the door to the checkerboard tiles and spangled sombreros inside, the

restaurant is playful and the food is genuine northern Mexican (*not* Tex-Mex). Lots of Mexican beers are available, but this is definitely a family restaurant, not a macho taco joint. Open Monday through Thursday 5:00 to 11:00 P.M., Friday and Saturday 11:00 A.M. to midnight, Sunday noon to 11:00 P.M. Inexpensive.

Wonder Spice Cafe,
697 Centre Street,
Jamaica Plain;
(617) 522–0200.
Essentially a Cambodian restaurant in Thai clothing (Thai is more recognizable to most people), Wonder Spice displays the French colonial influence and subtle spicing typical of Cambodian food. Many vegetarian options are available. The hard part is getting a seat. Open for lunch Monday through Friday 11:30 A.M. to 3:30 P.M., Saturday and Sunday 11:50 A.M. to 3:30 P.M., for dinner Sunday through Thursday 5:00 to 10:00 P.M., Friday and Saturday 5:00 to 10:30 P.M. Inexpensive.

Zaftig's Delicatessen,
335 Harvard Street,
Brookline;
(617) 975–0075;
www.zaftigs.com.
From a hearty Reuben to a plate of sliced tongue with potato salad, Zaftig's is a gemütlich cross between a Jewish grandmother's Brooklyn kitchen and a hard-boiled New York deli. You could do worse. Open daily 8:00 A.M. to 10:00 P.M. Inexpensive.

Cambridge

We dyed-in-the-wool Cantabrigians consider Cambridge to be Boston's younger, smarter sister. Founded in 1631, "Newtowne" assumed its true identity in 1636, when the Massachusetts Bay Colony chose the village for a college "to advance Learning and perpetuate it to Posterity; dreading to leave an illiterate Ministry to the Churches, when our present Ministers shall lie in the Dust." Two years later, Charlestown cleric John Harvard went to his reward, leaving half his modest fortune and all of his books to the college. His legacy might be the best buy in the history of charitable "naming": The legislators voted to call the school Harvard College and rechristen the town as Cambridge, in honor of the English university city.

Since those Puritan days, Cambridge has grown into the second most densely populated city in the United States (after New York), with extensive ethnic neighborhoods, vigorous high-tech and knowledge industries, and another world-class university—the Massachusetts Institute of Technology.

Harvard Square and Yard

From the outset, the heart of Cambridge has been the winding network of streets around Harvard Square, the most *on*-the-

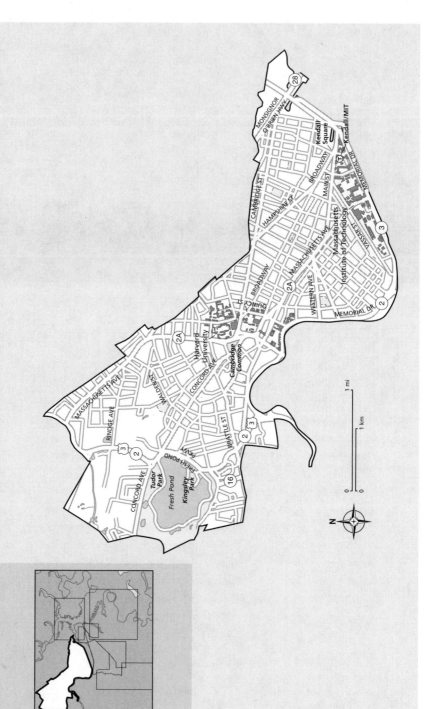

beaten-path quadrant of the city. Unless you have a masochistic tolerance for vehicular frustration, arrive in Harvard Square via the MBTA subway's Red Line.

As you trudge up the steps from darkness into light, the plaza above swirls with pedantry, sophistry, and mendicancy. In short, Harvard Square is full of itself, and its self-importance is part of its charm.

On the first Thursday in June, Harvard holds its annual commencement ceremonies. Perhaps it's because the school was founded to train ministers, but good weather is virtually assured for that date, as if by Divine compact. Immediately thereafter, however, the air clouds as Harvard alumni descend on Cambridge for their reunions and universally gripe that Harvard Square just isn't what it used to be.

we are family

Cambridge's international sister cities include Bulawayo, Zimbabwe; Yerevan, Armenia; Galway, Ireland; and Tsukuba, Japan.

schoolcolors

The MBTA's Red Line subway was designated with that color to denote its original terminus at Harvard, where the school's color is crimson.

As a matter of fact, it's *exactly* what it has always been since late 1630s, when the first brewery was licensed here, giving students an excuse to congregate and spend their money. Harvard Square is the unapologetic mercantile heart of Cambridge, where students, teachers, and those who emulate them come to shop. Few places are blessed with so many independent bookstores. And while some stalwart defenders of the three-story, redbrick version of the square weep for the demise of small record shops and the creeping incursion of chain stores, Harvard Square offers exhaustive selections of recorded music at Tower Records.

Once you've traipsed the stores on Mass. Ave. (as locals call Massachusetts Avenue) and on JFK and Brattle Streets, and strolled through the leafy groves of academe (Harvard Yard—right behind those walls) and perhaps even visited Harvard's art museums, you're ready to uncover some of the lesser-known gems of America's oldest university.

boom or busk

Street performers have always hung out in Harvard Square, but with advances in portable sound systems, their noise pollution became such a serious problem that the City Council established an ordinance in 1990 limiting their volume to eighty decibels to settle what musicians were calling "the volume wars."

openingtunes

Among the successful musicians who got their start singing on the streets of Harvard Square are Joan Baez, Tracy Chapman, and Bonnie Raitt.

Even hard-core museum- and gallery-goers often overlook the **Carpenter Center for the Visual Arts** at 21 Quincy Street, right next door to the Fogg Art Museum. Constructed in 1963, this structure of intersecting planes and curves is a landmark of modern architecture. It's the only building in North America by the French architect, painter, and sculptor Le Corbusier, who taught briefly at Harvard. To fully appreciate the swirling transitions of the Carpenter Center, stroll up the curving exterior walkway on Quincy Street to the glass-box rooms that make up the **Sert Gallery,** where you'll find changing exhibitions of contemporary art curated by the Harvard Art Museums. The gallery is named for another famous modern architect who also taught at Harvard, the Catalan master Josep Lluis Sert. The gallery is open Monday through Saturday 10:00 A.M. to 5:00 P.M., Sunday noon to 5:00 P.M. Free admission. Call (617) 495–3251; www.art museums.harvard.edu/sert/.

separatebutequal?

W.E.B. DuBois was the first African American to receive a Ph.D. at Harvard, graduating in 1895. He was not welcome in the Harvard dormitories, so he rented a room at 20 Flagg Street. "I was in Harvard, but not of it," he later wrote.

Adjacent to the gallery, the **Sert Gallery Café** has a limited but imaginative menu of wrap sandwiches (curried chicken or goat cheese and white bean), salads (Greek, Caesar, Asian, chicken), and soups (carrot ginger), as well as sweets. In nice weather, try to grab one of the tables on the outside deck, where you can gaze on the polychrome tower of Memorial Hall. The bronze sculpture in the cafe—a pyramid of donkey, dog, cat, and cock—was created in 1951 by Gerhard Marcks and refers to a nineteenth-century folktale.

beauregardwho?

Harvard's Memorial Hall is dedicated to the 136 Harvard men who died for the Union cause in the Civil War, but it does not acknowledge the sixty-four Harvard men who perished fighting for the Confederacy.

It's much more whimsical and traditional than anything that you will likely find in the gallery.

The lowest level of Carpenter Center houses film projection rooms as well as the **Harvard Film Archives (HFA).** Visitors rarely hear about this particular treasure, but the HFA owns more

Well-Versed

In this digital age when most books can be ordered online for overnight delivery, the *Grolier Poetry Book Shop* continues to hand-sell slim little volumes you'd be hard-pressed to find anywhere else in America—maybe even anywhere else in the world. Proprietor Louisa Solano wedges 15,000 titles into a shop the size of a small cafe, carrying the torch for the first and most enduring form of literature. The Grolier, at 6 Plympton Street, is open Monday to Saturday noon to 6:30 P.M. (sometimes closing at 6:00 P.M. on Tuesdays or Saturdays for poetry readings or autograph parties). Call (617) 547–4648.

than 3,000 classic and experimental films from around the world. If multiplex movies make you yawn, you can attend a more challenging screening almost every night of the year at the Carpenter Center. Presentations range from student films to current art films to classics to popular films. Admission: adults $8.00, students and seniors $6.00. Call (617) 495–4700; www.harvardfilmarchive.org.

Reenter Harvard Yard across Quincy Street from the Carpenter Center and walk down to the corner of the long steps of Widener Library. Look to your left for the public entrance for the Pusey Library, home of the **Harvard Map Collection** (617–495–2417) and the **Harvard Theatre Collection** (617–495–2445). Antiquarian maps have been a focus of Harvard since the college was founded in 1636, and the collections of pre-1900 maps, atlases, and nautical charts are unparalleled. You'll even see a 1541 globe of the world (admittedly somewhat erroneous) as drawn by Gerhard Mercator of Antwerp. The Theatre Collection is one of America's earliest aggregations of artifacts for performing arts research, and the photographs and negatives of stage productions are show-stoppers. Curators mount small exhibitions so that non-scholars can sample the archival riches. The Theatre Collection is open Monday through Friday 1:00 to 4:45 P.M. The Map Collection is open Monday through Friday 10:00 A.M. to 4:00 P.M.

Continue past the entrance to the Pusey Library and bear left to reach the entrance of the **Houghton Library,** repository of some of the university's greatest treasures. The library holds more than ten million manuscripts (including some dating back to 3,000 BCE) as well as 500,000 books from the fifteenth century forward. In addition to books printed in England and the United States, the collection includes books in French, Italian,

readinglist

There are more than 4.5 million books on more than 5 miles of shelves in Harvard's Widener Library.

German, Russian, Dutch, Scandinavian, Portuguese, Spanish, and modern Greek. Highlights of the collection are usually on display in an elegant first-floor hall with glass-front bookshelves on all four walls. The library is open Monday through Friday from 9:00 A.M. to 5:00 P.M. and Saturday from 9:00 A.M. to 1:00 P.M. Free tours are given on Fridays at 2:00 P.M. Call (617) 495–2440.

Before you leave Harvard Yard, scan the bulletin boards for announcements of events open to the public. During the academic year there's a busy schedule of movies, concerts, lectures, and theater performances, often free or with very modest admission prices.

Outside the walls of Harvard Yard, above the Cambridge Street underpass, is a broad plain with a fountain that sprays water in warm weather and steam in cold weather. The dramatic modern building behind the plain is the Harvard Science Center. In a lower-level gallery, the **Collection of Historic Scientific Instruments** represents the laboratory and classroom devices of yesteryear at Harvard, which has been purchasing such equipment since 1764. The official collection was inaugurated in 1947 and has grown to include more than 15,000 objects that date from 1450 to the present. The small exhibition space, visible through glass walls even when it's closed, holds an array of beautifully wrought precision instruments whose technical obsolescence does not detract from their exacting beauty. Some of the most fascinating pieces are astronomical, such as a French planispheric astrolabe (circa 1450) or one of Harvard's first telescopes, purchased in 1767 upon the advice of Benjamin Franklin. The Science Center is at 1 Oxford Street. The building is open around the clock, but the gallery is open Monday through Friday 9:00 A.M. to 5:00 P.M. It sometimes closes unexpectedly, so call ahead. Call (617) 495–2627. Free admission.

If you walk up Kirkland Street from the Science Center and turn left on Divinity Avenue (a good route to get to the famous Peabody Museum of

Ticket to Savings

If you get really ambitious and decide to visit all of Harvard's major museums, you can save money on admission by purchasing the **Harvard Hot Ticket,** which costs $10.00 for adults and $8.00 for seniors and college students. It's good for the Arthur M. Sackler Museum (ancient, Asian, Islamic, and Later Indian art), the Busch-Reisinger Museum (art of Germany, Austria, and other northern European cultures), the Fogg Art Museum (with a survey of art from the Middle Ages to the present), the Harvard Museum of Natural History (the Glass Flowers, as well as minerals, meteorites, dinosaur skeletons, and taxidermied animals), and the Peabody Museum of Archaeology and Ethnology (which has holdings from six continents). The Semitic Museum—which does not charge admission—is also on the pass.

Archaeology and Ethnology), you'll find the tiny **Semitic Museum,** an *Indiana Jones/ English Patient* kind of place. Under the museum's aegis, scholars and excavators have plumbed the secrets of the ancient Near East. There's an air of great romance about the excavations of the Egyptian pyramids or the amazing discovery of the great cosmopolitan city of Niza, buried beneath the sands of modern Iraq for more than 4,000 years. The Semitic Museum is at 6 Divinity Avenue. Open Monday through Friday 10:00 A.M. to 4:00 P.M., Sunday 1:00 to 4:00 P.M., closed Saturday. Call (617) 495–4631. Free admission.

fragilebeauty

The 4,000 glass botanical models known as "the Glass Flowers" were laboriously hand-blown by father-and-son glassblowers Leopold and Rudolf Blashka in Dresden, Germany, between 1887 and 1936. They are housed at the Harvard Botanical Museum, 26 Oxford Street, (617) 495–3045. Open Monday through Saturday 9:00 A.M. to 5:00 P.M., Sunday 1:00 to 5:00 P.M. Admission is $7.50. From September to May, admission is free on Sunday from 9:00 A.M. to noon and Wednesday from 3:00 to 5:00 P.M.

Cambridge's own history seems almost modern by comparison. When you've finished exploring Harvard's arcane corners, return to Harvard Square to stroll along Brattle Street to the Hooper-Lee-Nichols House, the oldest house in the city and one of our favorite outings with out-of-town guests. Brattle Street is also known as **Tory Row,** since many of the rich merchants who lived here remained loyal to King George and were forced to flee during the Revolution. The mile-long route is dotted with blue oval historical markers identifying significant buildings.

The **William Brattle House** at 42 Brattle Street was built in 1727 for the prominent physician, preacher, lawyer, and Colonial attorney-general. The modest frame house, now host to the Cambridge Center for Adult Education, was confiscated in the Revolution and served as headquarters for the Continental Army's commissary general. A few doors down you'll come to the home of the village blacksmith celebrated in Henry Wadsworth Longfellow's poem. ("Under the spreading chestnut tree the village smithy stands. . . . ") Today the **Dexter Pratt House** (1808) at 54 Brattle Street houses **Hi-Rise Bakery,** but walk into the courtyard to see the forged-steel chestnut tree sculpture on the brick wall facing the house.

Many people never go any farther down Brattle than the **Loeb Drama Center** at 64 Brattle Street, home of the American Repertory Theatre. But Brattle is one of the most beautiful streets of American domestic architecture, and it's worth taking a stroll. Not all the landmarks are Colonial-era mansions. Handsome as a landlocked ocean liner, the **Stoughton House** at 90 Brattle

Street was designed by H. H. Richardson in 1882. It's one of the definitive houses in the Shingle style. A high fence makes it hard to see from the street, but you can get a good appreciation of its genteel mass from the driveway.

At the corner of Hawthorne Street stands another confiscated Tory home, the **Henry Vassall House** (94 Brattle Street). The center of the structure, with its 8-foot square chimney, dates from the seventeenth century, but like many New Englanders, the Vassalls kept adding onto the structure right up to 1775, when they fled to England. Their house was the Continental Army's medical headquarters during the Siege of Boston (1775–76).

There's no missing the **Longfellow Historical Site** at 105 Brattle Street, a Tory manse that served as George Washington's headquarters and later became the home of poet, translator, and Harvard professor Henry Wadsworth Longfellow. Across Brattle Street from the house is Longfellow Park. Down the west side, at number 5, is the redbrick **Friends Meeting House (Quaker),** with Sunday meetings at 10:30 A.M. and 5:00 P.M. For information, call (617) 876–6883 or e-mail at FMCQUAKER@aol.com.

Walk down a few steps into the lower portion of Longfellow Park, which fronts on Memorial Drive and the Charles River, for the stately monument to the Good Gray Poet. Longfellow's bronze bust is flanked by bas-reliefs of some of his most memorable characters: Miles Standish, Beatrice, and Dante on the left; Evangeline and Gabriel and Hiawatha on the right.

About a quarter-mile farther out Brattle Street, the **Hooper-Lee-Nichols House** at 159 Brattle Street dates from 1688, making it the oldest house standing in the city. Now home of the Cambridge Historical Society, this farmhouse remodeled as a mansion is open for tours on Tuesday and Thursday 2:00 to 5:00 P.M. Admission is $5.00. Call (617) 547–4252.

Double back on Brattle Street a short distance to Craigie Street and turn left to wander a delightful neighborhood of handsome Colonial, Federal, and

Stargazers

If a huge asteroid ever ends up on a collision course with Earth, chances are Cambridge will know about it first. The **Harvard-Smithsonian Center for Astrophysics (CfA)** at 60 Garden Street serves as the headquarters for the Central Bureau for Astronomical Telegrams and the Minor Planet Center of the International Astronomical Union, coordinating sightings of new comets, asteroids, and other solar system debris.

At 8:00 P.M. on the third Thursday of each month, weather permitting, the CfA also holds public observing nights with lectures and stargazing in Phillips Auditorium. The 1912 telescope on the roof was recently refurbished and reveals the planets in great color and detail. Doors open at 7:30 P.M. Call (617) 495–7461.

Hooper-Lee-Nichols House

Victorian homes. If it's late in the day, you might want to stop for dinner at **Craigie Street Bistrot** at 5 Craigie Street; (617) 497–5511. The chef trained in neighborhood restaurants in Lyon, France, and, in keeping with that country's bistrot movement, he updates classic recipes to make them lighter and fresher. Cross Concord Street and turn right, then cross Garden Street to have a look at the buildings of the superb **Longy School of Music.** The music school, founded in 1915, occupies a wonderful brownstone-and-brick structure in the Richardsonian Romanesque style. Wedded to the older structure is the surprisingly complementary modern building that houses the **Edward Pickman Concert Hall,** where free or inexpensive concerts of small ensembles are offered a few times per week. Call (617) 876–0956 for information.

Cross Waterhouse Street to **Cambridge Common,** the sixteen-acre remnant of the original eighty-six acres set aside in 1631 for grazing and public activities. In 1775 this town cow pasture and drill ground became the encampment for 10,000 volunteer soldiers of the Continental Army who had converged on Cambridge to lay siege to Boston, held by British regulars. Note the plaque on the south side of the common, beneath a scion of the **Washington Elm.** Tradition holds that George Washington of Virginia took com-

remembrance of things past

Dedicated in 1997, the *Memorial to Irish Famine* on Cambridge Common was the first such memorial erected in the United States.

Among the Hallowed Dead

Mount Auburn Cemetery changed the American way of death, replacing the austere practicality of Colonial graveyards with a beautiful woodland burial ground that makes you glad to be alive. Founded in 1831 by the Massachusetts Horticultural Society on what was then a woodsy patch far out of the city, the 174-acre Mount Auburn Cemetery continues to operate as a burial ground, though empty plots are few and far between.

If you love cultivated plantings or like to watch birds, Mount Auburn is a "must" stop. More than 300 species of trees and 130 species of shrubs and ground covers provide sanctuary for urban wildlife, including more than eighty species of spring migratory birds. During the peak migration (mid-May), as many as 1,000 birders per day visit Mount Auburn and a "Bird Sightings" bulletin board is posted at the Brattle Street gatehouse.

About 87,000 people lie at rest along 10 miles of roads and paths. Ask for a map and walking tour guide at the main gate if you want to pay homage to such notables as navigator Nathaniel Bowditch, architect Charles Bulfinch, Christian Science founder Mary Baker Eddy (no, there is no telephone in her tomb), artist Winslow Homer, Polaroid inventor Edwin Land, and poet Henry Wadsworth Longfellow.

The main entrance to Mount Auburn Cemetery is at 580 Mount Auburn Street, about 3 miles west of Harvard Square toward Watertown. (Drive or take the no. 71 bus from Harvard Square.) Open daily 8:00 A.M. to 7:00 P.M. Call (617) 547–7105.

mand of the Continental Army beneath the original elm (which toppled in a 1923 hurricane) on July 3, 1775. Through the winter of 1775–76, the American forces huddled here, faring far better than they would at Valley Forge a few years later. Come spring, Washington out-maneuvered the British forces and forced their withdrawal from Boston. If the American soldiers had any idea what hardships awaited them, they probably left Cambridge with the greatest reluctance.

Today the common is a park with ball fields and grassy patches, ideal for reading in the shade of an old tree. In the center you will see a landmark characteristic of most towns and cities in New England, the *Civil War Memorial* to the soldiers and sailors "who gave their lives in the war to preserve the union." The bronze of Abraham Lincoln in the center of the memorial was a later addition to the granite monument. It's a casting of the standing Lincoln that Augustus Saint-Gaudens sculpted for Chicago.

Toward Porter Square

Across Massachusetts Avenue from Cambridge Common is Harvard Law School, with its romantic landmark building, *Austin Hall,* designed by H. H. Richardson and built between 1881 and 1883. Austin Hall shows Richardson at his most flamboyant, trimming the dark local sandstone with pale yellow Ohio stone and decorating the facade with bluestone marquetry. Pop in to see the fireplace in the James Barr Ames Courtroom, originally the library. The fireplace is so exquisite that it is, by itself, a National Historic Landmark.

precious gas

The neon *Shell* sign on the corner of Magazine Street and Memorial Drive was designated a historic landmark by the Cambridge Historical Commission, which cited it as an "artifact of a vanishing era and landscape."

Walking up Massachusetts Avenue toward Porter Square, you'll encounter a quirky collection of shops; easy-going cafes, restaurants, and bars; and a handful of entertainment spots. Many Cambridge residents feel that this stretch of Mass. Ave. retains the verve that Harvard Square has lost over the years.

From the exterior, you'd think that **Montrose Spa** at 1646 Massachusetts Avenue (617–547–5053) is just another neighborhood convenience store, but the Cuban owners stock Caribbean produce and specialty products for their loyal clientele. The secret ingredient in their Cubano sandwiches (arguably the best around Boston) is the Cuban-style roast pork imported from New York. Open daily 7:00 A.M. to 11:00 P.M.

Just as Harvard Square had the old Club 47 (now Club Passim) during the 1960s "folk scare," Upper Mass. Ave. has the **Lizard Lounge** at 1667 Massachusetts Avenue (617–547–0759) for the new millennium. This basement bar is one of the hippest venues for up-and-coming singer-songwriters and performance poets. Figures from headliner bands on tour sometimes stop in for a solo acoustic act on a rainy midweek night. You never know. Entertainment begins Sunday at 7:00 P.M., Monday at 8:00 P.M., Tuesday and Wednesday at 8:30 P.M., Thursday through Saturday at 9:00 P.M.

Is it a shop or a mini-museum of twentieth-century design? Visit **Abodeon** at 1731 Massachusetts Avenue (617–497–0137) if you're an aficionado of modern design. The changing selection of vintage housewares, jewelry, small furniture,

Art on the Line

A 20-foot-high red kinetic sculpture, Gift of the Wind, marks the **Porter Square MBTA station** from a good quarter mile away. But you'll have to buy a token to see the local favorite piece of public art in the subway system—Mags Harries' *Glove Cycle* from 1985. Life-size bronze gloves are scattered throughout the station as if dropped by commuters.

and lighting fixtures is augmented by a few new items that share a similar design aesthetic (most of them from Scandinavia, where "Danish Modern" still runs strong). The new merchandise is identified by the year in which it was designed and by the name of the designer. Open Monday through Wednesday 10:00 A.M. to 6:00 P.M., Thursday through Saturday 10:00 A.M. to 7:00 P.M., Sunday noon to 6:00 P.M.

If modern design leaves you cold, you can turn instead to **Nomad** for colorful folk art accessories for your home. You can buy enough Mexican tiles to cover a wall, or select individual accent pieces such as carved wooden animals, colorful ceramic serving dishes, elegant Japanese sake sets, Near Eastern kilims, and even clever South African objects made of recycled tin cans. Nomad is located at 1741 Massachusetts Avenue (617–497–6677) and is open Monday, Tuesday, and Saturday 10:00 A.M. to 6:00 P.M.; Wednesday through Friday 10:00 A.M. to 7:00 P.M.; and Sunday noon to 6:00 P.M.

Fans of Arlington-based clothing designer Deborah Parker descend on **Susanna** at 1776 Massachusetts Avenue (617–492–0334), which carries a selection of Parker's simple, elegant, and wearable skirts, pants, tops, and dresses in attractive and slightly unusual fabrics. The small shop offers friendly, unpressured service and advice on accessorizing. Open Monday through Saturday 10:00 A.M. to 6:00 P.M. (Thursday until 8:00 P.M.), Sunday noon to 5:00 P.M.

Paper Source has just about anything you can think of related to paper—wrapping paper in distinctive designs, stationery and envelopes in a range of colors, fountain pens and inks, stamps and stickers, and a wide choice of albums, including some especially for weddings. Paper Source is at 1810 Massachusetts Avenue (617–497–1077) and is open Monday through Friday 10:00 A.M. to 7:00 P.M., Saturday 10:00 A.M. to 6:00 P.M., and Sunday 11:00 A.M. to 5:00 P.M.

The landmark on the corner of Massachusetts Avenue and Upland Road is the **Porter Exchange Building,** 1815 Massachusetts Avenue. The former Sears, Roebuck, building has a striking Art Deco facade and is now partly filled with Lesley and Harvard University offices. But Porter Exchange has also evolved as a magnet for Asian students and other lovers of Japanese food and products. In the central atrium, a **Shiseido** counter carries a full range of skincare products. It's open Monday through Saturday 11:00 A.M. to 7:00 P.M., Sunday noon to 6:00 P.M. **Tokai** gift shop (617–864–5922) proffers many attractive Japanese items, including kimonos, ceramics, calligraphy sets, origami materials, and instructions. Tokai is open Monday through Saturday 10:30 A.M. to 7:30 P.M., Sunday noon to 5:30 P.M.

But most people come to the Porter Exchange Building to eat at the

Japanese restaurants and fast-food counters. The casual spots—such as *Kotobukiya* (617–492–4655) for sushi and *Sapporo Ramen* (617–876–4805) for noodle dishes—are crowded and lively. For a more relaxed meal, try *Blue Fin* (617–497–8022). Inexpensive lunch specials tend toward pan-fried vegetables and tofu and teriyaki dishes. Dinner "sets" are more exotic. Plates might include grated mountain yam with tuna sashimi or one of our favorites, *yosen-abe* (a heaping serving of seafood, chicken, vegetables, and tofu simmered in a mild fish broth). Restaurants tend to be open daily from 10:30 A.M. to 10:00 P.M., with an hour out for prep time between 4:00 and 5:00 P.M.

Across from the subway station, the Porter Square Shopping Center has a large parking lot where non-shoppers will definitely be towed. Along the White Street side of the lot is the Marketplace at Porter Square, where *Mudflat Gallery* (617–491–7976) serves as an outlet for the works of the talented members of a ceramics cooperative in nearby Somerville. Decorative and functional ceramics are available in a wide range of styles and prices. Open Monday through Saturday 10:00 A.M. to 7:00 P.M., Sunday noon to 6:00 P.M.

Additional amusements await farther up Mass. Ave. Up-and-coming local acts perform with ear-splitting volume at the narrow, tiny bar called *Toad* at 1920 Massachusetts Avenue (617–497–4950), where there's live music seven nights a week with no cover charge. Toad is open Monday through Wednesday 5:00 P.M. to 1:00 A.M., Thursday through Saturday 5:00 P.M. to 2:00 A.M., Sunday 6:00 P.M. to 1:00 A.M. If you're curious about your future, your job, your love life, or your stock portfolio, stop in for a reading with *Mrs. Donna, Reader and Advisor,* who holds forth in the basement level of 1923 Massachusetts Avenue. Call ahead for an appointment (617–492–5044) for palm readings, tarot cards, crystal ball, horoscope charts, and other methods of divination. (Believe it or not, she doesn't know you're coming.)

MIT and Kendall Square

Harvard's crosstown rival is the Massachusetts Institute of Technology (MIT), as towering a force in the realms of science and engineering as Harvard is in the humanities and social sciences. Spread mostly as low and squat as a mushroom patch along the Charles River between the Longfellow and Harvard bridges (Broadway/Main Street and Massachusetts Avenue, respectively), "Tech" is a relative latecomer to Cambridge, moving here in 1909 after outgrowing Copley Square.

As Cantabrigians we're always amazed at the thousands of people who hop the Red Line to Harvard Square and subject themselves to the Harvard College tour, yet never stop at Kendall Square to visit the *MIT campus.* Even for those of us who live here, MIT is one of those places you often pass and rarely stop. We've heard of the "hacks" (such as parking an MIT police car on top of the dome), but we've never been inside the school itself to see where such strange minds develop.

MIT had one of America's first schools of architecture, and the campus is a showpiece of movements from neoclassicism to postmodernism, with a heaping dose of mid-twentieth-century Modernism that seems exactly right for a school in the vanguard of technology. Some of the giants of modern architecture have contributed to the campus.

MIT offers a twice-daily campus tour. We've never seen anyone on the tour except prospective students and their parents, perhaps because the student tour leaders concentrate on recruiting applicants. But they will also tolerate those of us simply curious about this parallel universe. (Visiting MIT can be a little like walking in on a *Star Trek* convention.) Free tours depart from the domed Rogers Building at 77 Massachusetts Avenue at 10:45 A.M. and 2:45 P.M. Monday through Friday and last about ninety minutes. Call (617) 253–4795.

The tour sets off down the **Infinite Corridor,** a $\frac{1}{6}$-mile hallway linking several buildings. Legend says that the sun shines straight down its length one day each in May and October. Almost all MIT buildings are connected, either above or below ground, and the sight of 10,000 students scurrying through MIT's 7 miles of tunnel-like corridors could put you in mind of an ant farm.

The tour whirls through laboratories, libraries, computer terminal rooms, and a lecture hall that served as the model for the math lecture hall in the movie *Good Will Hunting.* Then you'll traipse through the most picturesque part of the outdoor MIT campus. You'll meander past Alexander Calder's massive but graceful sculpture *The Big Sail,* around the gusty base of Green Hall (the tallest

The Mystery beyond Porter Square

It was eating at Marlowe that he didn't know what he needed to know. Maybe it was the conk on the head or the distraction when the blonde with orchid-red lipstick flashed a little ankle as she got into the unmarked car. One thing he did know: Kate would have the goods. If he knew what was good for him, he'd better see Kate.

Every detective's best friend in Cambridge, Kate Mattes, operates **Kate's Mystery Books** at 2211 Massachusetts Avenue. It's a bit of a schlep beyond Porter Square, but where else can you find a bookstore where Spenser's creator, Robert Parker, built the shelves? The shop is jammed with new and used mysteries, suspense novels, and a few less–easily categorized books that strike Kate's fancy. Open Monday to Friday noon to 7:00 P.M., Thursday noon to 8:00 P.M., Saturday 11:00 A.M. to 5:00 P.M., and Sunday noon to 5:00 P.M. Call (617) 491–2660; www.katesmysterybooks.com.

structure in Cambridge and, appropriately, home to planetary and atmospheric sciences), and into the green lawns of Killian Court, the Versailles-like swath of nature between the Charles River and the majestic Ionic columns and Great Dome of the Maclaurin building.

@cambridge

The engineering consulting firm of Bolt, Beranek & Newman, then headquartered in Kendall Square, was one of the designers of Arpanet, the predecessor of the Internet. The firm is credited with sending the first e-mail message in the 1970s.

MIT students are invariably photographed in front of the Great Dome during orientation sessions and at graduation. In between, they spend warm, sunny days lounging in the grass, playing Frisbee, or plotting some new prank, like the legendary stunt of hoisting an MIT police car atop the dome, complete with a dummy policeman chomping a doughnut. Walk around the corner (past the Henry Moore statue), and you're suddenly back on Mass. Ave.

There are three interesting MIT destinations that the official tour skips. These are the Hart Nautical Gallery, the MIT Museum, and the List Visual Art Center.

Inside the Rogers Building, an extraordinary collection of model ships is displayed under glass in the ***Hart Nautical Gallery.*** MIT has dealt with nautical and oceanographic engineering from its founding, and these ships represent some design landmarks in the history of naval architecture. Among them are a model of the *Flying Cloud,* the record-setting clipper ship built by Donald McKay in East Boston in 1851; the famous British clipper *Cutty Sark;* and some of the vessels that explored New England's coast in the sixteenth and seventeenth centuries. The gallery is open daily 9:00 A.M. to 8:00 P.M. Free admission.

Before you leave the Rogers Building, climb the stairs to the second floor to the ***Rotch Architecture Library,*** where a small exhibit area often displays

Glad Rags

On the days leading up to Halloween, every hipster in Boston hops the Red Line to Kendall and hikes over the railroad tracks to 200 Broadway (617–876–5230) for the strangest used-clothing store in town. The **Garment District** resembles the Salvation Army cubed—a funky second-story warehouse of vintage and downright weird used clothing, relics of various counterculture fads. Open Sunday through Tuesday 11:00 A.M. to 7:00 P.M., Wednesday through Friday 11:00 A.M. to 8:00 P.M., Saturday 9:00 A.M. to 7:00 P.M. Downstairs, **Dollar a Pound** has all sorts of flea market and attic castoffs: heaps of clothing at literally $1.00 per pound and old LPs and CDs—cheap. Open Sunday, Monday, and Tuesday 9:00 A.M. to 7:00 P.M., Wednesday and Thursday 9:00 A.M. to 8:00 P.M., and Friday and Saturday 9:00 A.M. to 7:00 P.M.

The Harvard Bridge from MIT to Boston

The *Mass. Ave. bridge* that links MIT to Boston may be named the Harvard Bridge, but Tech students have put their mark on it. The span is measured in units called "smoots," based on a 1958 survey in which Lambda Chi Alpha pledge Oliver R. Smoot was laid end to end as a human yardstick. The bridge is 364.4 smoots and one ear long.

students' thesis projects. Few people are aware that MIT has a strong program in the visual arts and that students and faculty members are often pioneers in exploring the intersection between art and technology. While you're on the second floor, you'll also be able to take a closer look at the massive dome, inspired by the Parthenon. The library is open Monday through Thursday 9:00 A.M. to 11:00 P.M., Friday 9:00 A.M. to 7:00 P.M., Saturday 11:00 A.M. to 6:00 P.M., and Sunday 2:00 to 10:00 P.M. Call (617) 258–5590.

The main gallery of the *MIT Museum* is located at 265 Massachusetts Avenue at the intersection of Front Street. The 2001 redesign of the museum has stripped away some of its original boyish fascination with simple gadgetry—gone are the cases of historic slide rules, the black-and-white photos of practical jokes in the "Hall of Hacks." But the museum has plenty to engage technophiles, from robots you can operate with buttons, levers, and dials to clever demonstrations of the practical applications of stroboscopic light. "Mind and Hand: The Making of MIT Scientists and Engineers" now dominates the space with a breathless account of the joys and exhilaration of an MIT education over the last century and a half. Admission is $5.00 for adults, $2.00 for

In the Middle of It All

The *Middle East* at 472 Massachusetts Avenue (617–492–1886) captures both ethnic dining and the hip music that makes Central Square, between Harvard and MIT, one of the top destinations in Boston for a little evening fun. This complex at the corner of Mass. Ave. and Brookline Street has it all—a casual Middle Eastern restaurant, a classy and upscale bistro with a Lebanese accent called ZuZu, a bakery, and not one but two music clubs. A sizable portion of Boston bohemia seems to more or less live here, but the big excitement comes when a new band lets it rip in the downstairs club, a converted bowling alley. We have a friend in Ohio who drove all the way to Cambridge to watch her favorite new band make its professional debut here. There's also traditional belly dancing every Wednesday night. Open daily from 11:00 A.M. to 1:00 A.M. (2:00 A.M. Thursday through Saturday). Call (617) 492–5162 for ticket information.

The Great Dome at MIT

seniors and students, $1.00 for children under 18. Call (617) 253–4444; web .mit.edu/museum.

Although the MIT Museum displays some rather magical art—three-dimensional holography and "Doc" Edgerton's photographs, for example—Tech's main art gallery is on the Kendall Square side of campus at the **List Visual Arts Center.** Here, exhibitions are often devoted to large-scale installations and conceptual art. The center sells an excellent annotated guide, *Art and Architecture at MIT: A Walking Tour of Campus.* Located at 20 Ames Street, the List is open October through June, Tuesday through Sunday noon to 6:00 P.M. (Friday until 8:00 P.M.). Admission is free. Call (617) 253–4680.

Stroll down Ames Street toward the Kendall Square MBTA station to experience what's left of the most elusive of Cambridge's "squares." Nearly a century ago, Kendall was among America's leading industrial centers, but by the mid-twentieth century it had become a low-lying wasteland of decaying buildings and empty lots. As MIT spread back from the Charles River, Kendall Square developed into a center for new digital and biotech companies that have nearly obscured the old square. Former mill buildings along the rail tracks on the Broadway side have emerged as **One Kendall Square,** a bustling center for shopping, dining, and entertainment. The **Landmark Kendall Square Cinema** shows art, foreign, and independent feature films in a multiplex setting—the thinking person's alternative to mall movies. Call (617) 494–9800.

Places to Stay in Harvard Square

Cambridge Marriott,
2 Cambridge Center;
(617) 494–6600 or
(800) 228–9290.
Some of the rooms have good views of the Charles River in this well-run convention-type hotel, close to the Kendall T stop. Moderate to expensive.

Charles Hotel,
1 Bennett Street;
(617) 864–1200 or
(800) 882–1818.
Steps from Harvard Square, the Charles offers sleek luxury minus the overstuffed look. The service restaurant, Henrietta's Table, serves fresh-market cuisine based on New England tradition. Ask about weekend promotional rates. Moderate to expensive.

Harvard Square Hotel,
110 Mount Auburn Street;
(617) 864–5200.
This "hotel" started life as a nondescript motor lodge plunked in the middle of the square, but recent renovations with quality furnishings have lifted it above mere minimal lodging. Free e-mail kiosk in the lobby. Moderate.

Inn at Harvard,
1201 Massachusetts Avenue;
(617) 491–2222 or
(800) 222–8733.
Designed largely for the convenience and comfort of Harvard VIPs, this inn on the edge of Harvard Square has accommodations that resemble the well-furnished bedroom at home, augmented by the delightful lounge in the huge central atrium. Moderate to expensive.

The Mary Prentiss Inn,
6 Prentiss Street;
(617) 661–2929;
www.maryprentissinn.com.
This Greek Revival–style home, more than 150 years old, was originally a country estate. Set less than a block from Mass. Ave., the inn has a beautifully landscaped outdoor terrace and twenty guest rooms decorated with antiques. Some rooms have wood-burning fireplaces and Jacuzzis. Room 6 and suites 19 and 20 open onto the terrace. You can have breakfast on the terrace in nice weather or huddle by the parlor fireplace when it's cold outside. Inexpensive to moderate.

University Park Hotel at MIT,
20 Sidney Street;
(617) 577–0200;
www.hotelatmit.com.
For the truly wired, "Hotel@MIT" actively courts folks who love the dot-com lifestyle. Convenient to MIT and not much else, it's sleek and snazzy, as befits the price. Moderate to expensive.

Places to Eat in Harvard Square

Algiers Coffee House,
40 Brattle Street;
(617) 492–1557.
Something of a Cambridge institution with its Middle Eastern food, strong coffee, and upstairs smoking section, Algiers has a terrific midday buffet of salads, chickpeas, feta, and breads.

AUTHORS' FAVORITES IN CAMBRIDGE

Carpenter Center for the Visual Arts

Semitic Museum

Porter Exchange

Abodeon

Kate's Mystery Books

List Visual Arts Center

Mudflat Gallery

AUTHORS' FAVORITE PLACES TO EAT IN CAMBRIDGE

Chez Henri	Rhythm and Spice
Emma's Pizza	Rialto
L.A. Burdick Chocolates	Salts
Oleana	West Side Lounge

Open daily 8:00 A.M. to midnight. Inexpensive.

Atasca Restaurant,
50 Hampshire Street;
(617) 621–6991.
Superb and authentic Portuguese cuisine from the Azores and the mainland reigns at this smart newcomer in Kendall Square. Excellent Portuguese wine list. Open daily 11:30 A.M. to 11:00 P.M. Moderate.

Blue Fin,
Porter Exchange Building,
1815 Massachusetts Avenue;
(617) 497–8022.
See page 145 for full description.

Blue Room,
1 Kendall Square;
(617) 494–9034.
For years the Blue Room has been the place where Cambridge gourmets and digital hotshots rub elbows over some of the best grill-based cuisine in the city. Thanks to the efforts of the previous owner as an advocate for local agriculture, the restaurant gets the inside track on locally grown produce, special fish catches, and such delicacies as for-aged wild mushrooms. Yet all that precious attention to detail doesn't get in the way of simple, fresh tastes. It's an electric place to dine—nobody gets the blues at the Blue Room. Open Sunday to Thursday 5:30 to 10:00 P.M., Friday and Saturday 5:30 to 11:00 P.M., and for Sunday brunch 11:00 A.M. to 2:30 P.M.

Campo de' Fiore,
1352A Massachusetts Avenue;
(617) 354–3805.
Holyoke Center isn't just for Harvard folks. Head into the enclosed arcade for *pane romano*—long rectangles of flat bread available with toppings that range from nut spreads to sausage and cheese. Open Monday through Friday 8:00 A.M. to 8:00 P.M., Saturday 11:00 A.M. to 6:00 P.M. Closed Sunday. Inexpensive.

Casablanca,
40 Brattle Street;
(617) 876–0999.
Casablanca approaches Mediterranean cuisine from the oblique angle of North Africa. In other words, you can get a great cassoulet or savor spicy meatballs of lamb and bulgur wheat. The bar in the rear is a time-honored literary watering hole. Open for lunch daily from 11:30 A.M. to 2:30 P.M.; for dinner Sunday through Thursday from 5:30 to 10:00 P.M., Friday and Saturday from 5:30 to 11:00 P.M. Moderate to expensive.

Chez Henri,
1 Shepard Street;
(617) 354–8980.
The room has Parisian panache, the bar has an au courant buzz, and the French Provincial menu has a Cuban accent. The duck tamales are legendary. Reservations accepted for groups of six or more, but otherwise you'll want to get in line early. Open Monday through Thursday 6:00 to 10:00 P.M., Friday and Saturday 5:30 to 10:30 P.M., Sunday 5:30 to 9:00 P.M. Expensive.

Craigie Steet Bistrot,
5 Craigie Street;
(617) 497–5511.
See page 141 for full description.

Elephant Walk,
2067 Massachusetts Avenue;
(617) 492–6900;
www.elephantwalk.com.
Combining classical French and elegant Cambodian cuisines in a mix-and-match menu, Elephant Walk has shown that sophisticated gourmet cooking can appeal to everyone. You can purchase the restaurant's lemongrass sauce along with a recipe card to re-create the very popular *Poulet à la Citronelle* at home. Open Sunday through Thursday 5:00 to 10:00 P.M., Friday and Saturday 5:00 to 11:00 P.M. Moderate.

Emma's Pizza,
40 Hampshire Street;
(617) 864–8534.
Pizza "pi" (as in 3.1416 . . .) reaches gourmet status with the thin, crackerlike crust and such fancy toppings as goat cheese, caramelized onions, thyme-sautéed mushrooms, and fresh baby spinach. Take-out available. Open Tuesday through Friday 11:30 A.M. to 10:00 P.M., Saturday 4:00 to 10:00 P.M. Closed Sunday and Monday. Moderate.

Forest Cafe,
1682 Massachusetts Avenue;
(617) 661–7810.
Don't be daunted by the biker-bar atmosphere. Grab a booth on the left side, away from the bar, and enjoy startlingly good Oaxacan- and Yucatecan-style Mexican food. Open daily for lunch 11:30 A.M. to 2:30 P.M., for dinner Sunday through Thursday 5:30 to 10:00 P.M., Friday and Saturday 5:00 to 11:00 P.M. Inexpensive.

Iruña,
56 John F. Kennedy Street;
(617) 868–5633.
Hard to find because it's about 30 feet off JFK Street, this longtime Harvard favorite excels with Basque dishes. (*Iruña* is the Basque name for the town of Pamplona). Open for lunch Monday through Friday noon to 2:00 P.M., for dinner Monday through Thursday 6:00 to 9:00 P.M., Friday 6:00 to 10:00 P.M., Saturday 1:30 to 10:00 P.M. Closed Sunday. Moderate.

L. A. Burdick Chocolates,
52D Brattle Street;
(617) 491–4340.
Serving maybe the world's best hot chocolate (milk, dark, or white!), Burdick puts the decadently rich drink on ice for the summer. Open Tuesday through Saturday 8:00 A.M. to 11:00 P.M., Sunday and Monday 9:00 A.M. to 9:00 P.M.

Middle East,
472 Massachusetts Avenue;
(617) 492–1886.
See page 148 for full description.

Oleana,
134 Hampshire Street;
(617) 661–0505.
Few Boston chefs coax out the subtleties of the Arabic side of the Mediterranean as well as Ana Sortun, who gleefully weds Arabic almonds to Provençal herbs in a chicken dish. Her Basque-inspired plates are especially welcome in cold weather—venison with caramelized turnip tart, tuna

stew (*marmitako*), and rabbit-and-mushroom paella salad. Open Sunday through Thursday 5:30 to 10:00 P.M., Friday and Saturday 5:30 to 11:00 P.M. Moderate to expensive.

Rhythm and Spice,
315 Massachusetts Avenue;
(617) 497–0977.
You'll definitely feel "easy in the islands" at this Jamaican grill and bar, where the jerk pork has the classic aroma of smoky pimento/allspice wood and the back bar is loaded with a rainbow of rums. On Wednesday through Saturday nights, they push back the tables for reggae and ska dancing. Open Sunday 2:00 to 9:30 P.M., Monday through Wednesday 5:00 to 9:30 P.M., Thursday through Saturday 5:30 P.M. to 1:00 A.M. (dinner until 10:30 P.M.). Inexpensive.

Rialto,
Charles Hotel,
1 Bennett Street;
(617) 661–5050.
One of Greater Boston's top dining destinations. Chef Jody Adams draws on the cuisines of the Mediterranean basin for a signature style that marries strong herbs and perfect vegetables in supporting roles to the best local fish and meats. Open Monday through Friday 5:30 to 10:00 P.M., Saturday 5:30 to 11:00 P.M., and Sunday 5:30 to 9:00 P.M. Expensive.

Salts,
798 Main Street;
(617) 876–8444.
Chef Steven Rosen draws on the culinary inspirations of eastern and central

Europe for this exquisite and welcoming American bistro. One of his signature dishes is lamb smoked with black tea and rosemary. Open Tuesday through Saturday 5:30 to 10:00 P.M. Closed Sunday and Monday. Expensive.

Sandrine's Bistro,
8 Holyoke Street;
(617) 497–5300.
Sandrine's features the hearty dishes of the chef's native Alsace, including a homemade *choucroute garni*. Sandrine's signature dish is *flammekueche*, a flame-baked flat bread with toppings. (Just don't let the chef hear you call it "pizza.")

Open for lunch Monday through Saturday 11:30 A.M. to 2:30 P.M.; for dinner Monday through Saturday 5:30 to 10:00 P.M.; Sunday 5:30 to 9:30 P.M. Moderate to expensive.

Tanjore,
18 Eliot Street;
(617) 868–1900.
Tour the cuisines of India's regions at dinner, with an emphasis on the roasted meats of the Northwest. The luncheon buffet maintains the high standard at very low prices. Open for lunch daily 11:30 A.M. to 3:30 P.M., for dinner daily 4:30 to 11:00 P.M. Inexpensive.

West Side Lounge,
1680 Massachusetts Avenue;
(617) 441–5566.
If America had a neighborhood bistro tradition, West Side Lounge would be the epitome. Great local meat, fish, and produce gets friendly, French-influenced treatment in the kitchen—and your wallet gets a break. There's even a good, if small, wine list. Open daily 5:30 P.M. to 1:00 A.M. (kitchen closes at midnight). Moderate.

Appendix: Annual Events

Boston has hundreds of special events every year—too many to list here—but the following rundown gives you some of the city's leading festivals, shows, sporting events, and celebrations. Because the dates of some events vary from year to year, you should confirm the dates to avoid disappointment. Unless otherwise indicated, contact the City of Boston, Mayor's Office of Special Events and Tourism, City Hall Plaza at (617) 635–3911, or visit cityofboston.gov/mayor/spevents. The *Boston Globe*'s "Calendar" section on Thursdays also provides timely information on activities occurring within the next week.

JANUARY

First Day Concert. Boston Baroque orchestra performs at Sanders Theatre at Harvard University. (617) 484–9200.

JANUARY/FEBRUARY

Chinese New Year. Chinatown celebration with parade, lion and dragon dances, firecrackers, and food. (617) 482–3292.

Anthony Spinazzola Gala. Black-tie event includes samplings from 120 top New England chefs and more than ninety national and international vintners. (617) 344–4413.

Boston Wine Expo. Largest consumer event of its kind in the United States. Includes tastings, seminars, and cooking demonstrations. (877) 946–3976; www.wine-expos.com.

FEBRUARY

Bean Pot Hockey Tournament. Spirited rivalry among Boston College, Boston University, Harvard University, and Northeastern University hockey teams. (617) 624–1000.

MARCH

New England Flower Show. Nation's oldest annual flower exhibition covers five indoor acres of landscaped gardens. (617) 933–4900; www.masshort.org.

Saint Patrick's Day Parade. Parade through South Boston honors the Irish saint and commemorates the evacuation of Boston by the British. In 1995 the U.S. Supreme Court ruled that the parade sponsors could exclude gay, lesbian, and bisexual marchers on the basis of freedom of speech.

APRIL

Boston Marathon. World's oldest annual marathon draws elite runners from around the world as well as thousands of amateurs, all aiming to cross the finish line in front of the Boston Public Library. (617) 236–1652.

Patriots Day Parade. Parade from City Hall Plaza to Paul Revere Mall in the North End, where the start of Paul Revere's Midnight Ride is reenacted.

Boston Cyberarts Festival. Exhibitions and events highlight artists working in new technologies in all media. Held in odd-numbered years. (617) 524–8495 or www.bostoncyberarts.org.

Swan Boats. Every April the Swan Boats appear in the Public Garden Lagoon to begin another season of fanciful fifteen-minute cruises. (617) 522–1966.

MAY

Ducklings Day Parade. Retraces the route of the ducklings in the children's classic *Make Way for Ducklings* by Robert McCloskey. (617) 426–1885.

Hidden Gardens of Beacon Hill. Since 1929 the Beacon Hill Garden Club has sponsored this opportunity to tour gardens that can't be seen from the sidewalk. (617) 227–4392.

Lilac Sunday. It's a tradition to stroll among the 400 lilac bushes at the Arnold Arboretum on the third Sunday in May, but the fragrant blooms last from early May to late June. (617) 524–1717.

Street Performers Festival. Top street performers from around the world strut their stuff at Faneuil Hall Marketplace. (617) 523–1300 or www.faneuil hallmarketplace.com.

Walk for Hunger. This 20-mile walk is one of the oldest and largest pledge walks in the country. (617) 723–5000.

Boston Gay and Lesbian Film/Video Festival. Screenings are held at the Museum of Fine Arts. (617) 369–3300.

JUNE

Boston Globe Jazz Festival. Weeklong celebration features free outdoor performances and some ticketed events. (617) 267–4301 or www.bostonglobe.com/promotions/jazzfest.

Scooper Bowl. One of the largest ice-cream festivals in the nation is held at City Hall Plaza. (617) 632–3300.

Dragon Boat Festival. Competitors race intricately painted and carved boats along the Charles River. (617) 441–2884.

Commemoration of the Battle of Bunker Hill. Events include costumed reenactors, talks, and tours as well as a parade from the monument to the militia training field. (617) 242–5641.

BTW Unbound: Festival of New Plays. Workshop performances of new plays from around the country. (617) 824–8000 or www.maj.org.

JULY

Boston Harborfest. Weeklong event includes children's activities and a chowderfest. (617) 227–1528.

Boston Pops Fourth of July Concert and Fireworks. The concert and fireworks display on Independence Day draw the biggest crowds, but the Pops also presents several other free concerts on the Esplanade during July. (617) 266–1492.

Bastille Day Street Dance Festival. The French Library and Cultural Center sponsors a block party with food and dancing. (617) 912–0400.

Festival Betances. Music, dancing, food, and sports honor the Puerto Rican patriot Dr. Ramon Betances. (617) 927–1707.

JULY/AUGUST

Religious Festivals. Patron saints from the old country are honored with parades, music, and food almost every weekend in the North End.

AUGUST

Civil War Encampment. Fort Warren on Georges Island hosts more than 300 reenactors in period costumes. (617) 727–7676.

Caribbean-American Carnival. One of the country's largest festivals of its kind, with live music, dancing, and food.

August Moon Festival. Chinatown festival features Chinese opera, martial-arts demonstrations, traditional dance, food, and arts and crafts displays. (617) 482–3292.

Commonwealth Shakespeare. Free performances are held at the Parkman Bandstand on Boston Common. (617) 423–7600.

SEPTEMBER

Cambridge Artists Open Studios. More than fifty artists from throughout

Cambridge open their studios. (617) 349–4380.

Boston Film Festival. Roughly fifty feature films have their Boston debut over a ten-day period in mid-September. Many of the feature films are also making their world or U.S. premieres. (617) 266–2533.

SEPTEMBER–DECEMBER

Artists' Open Studios. Artists in a dozen Boston neighborhoods open their studios to visitors on weekends. (617) 635–3245.

OCTOBER

Art Newbury Street. Three-day event celebrates the art galleries on Newbury Street. (617) 267–2224.

Head of the Charles Regatta. World's largest two-day rowing event features more than 2,000 boats. (617) 868–6200 or www.hocr.org.

Oktoberfest. Traditional beer garden, live music, and food in Harvard Square. (617) 491–3434.

South End House Tour. A handful of domiciles in the largest Victorian brick row house neighborhood in the U.S. open for visitors each year. (617) 536–4445 or www.southendhistoricalsociety.org.

NOVEMBER

Frog Pond on the Boston Common opens for ice-skating season. (617) 635–2120.

Boston International Antiquarian Book Fair. One of the oldest and largest in the United States. (617) 266–6540 or www.bostonbookfair.com.

Ellis Memorial Antiques Show. Second-oldest charity antiques show in the country. (617) 248–8571.

Boston Jewish Film Festival. Showcases contemporary films with Jewish themes. (617) 824–8000.

DECEMBER

Reenactment of Boston Tea Party. Begins at Old South Meeting House and proceeds to the Tea Party Ship on the Congress Street Bridge. (617) 338–1773.

Christmas Lighting Ceremonies. Illumination of the 50-foot tree at the Prudential and of the lights on Boston Common are accompanied by music and other celebrations.

Jingle Bell Fun Run. Champion marathoner Bill Rodgers leads 2,000 runners in annual non-competitive 5K jog through Boston followed by a huge party to benefit charity. (617) 723–5612.

Christmas Performances. Seasonal favorites include the *Nutcracker* performed by the Boston Ballet (617–695–6950) and by José Mateo's Ballet Theatre (617–354–7467), Handel's *Messiah* performed by the Handel & Haydn Society (617–266–3605), Langston Hughes's gospel play *The Black Nativity* (617–824–8000), and *Christmas Revels* (617–972–8300).

First Night. Boston pioneered the multicultural, arts-based New Year's Eve celebration that has spread to more than 130 other cities. See Thursday *Boston Globe* "Calendar" for full schedule of indoor and outdoor activities, including a parade, fireworks, and lots of children's activities. (617) 542–1399 or www .firstnight.org.

Indexes

Entries for Restaurants, Lodgings, Museums/Historic Sites, and Parks/Outdoor Attractions appear in the special indexes beginning on page 163.

GENERAL INDEX

RESTAURANTS

LODGINGS

MUSEUMS/HISTORIC SITES

PARKS/OUTDOOR ATTRACTIONS

About the Authors

Patricia Harris and David Lyon have collaborated as essayists, travel journalists, and as art and restaurant critics since 1981. Their other books from the Globe Pequot Press include *Food Lovers' Guide to Massachusetts* and *Romantic Days & Nights in Boston*. Although they have lived in Cambridge for nearly fifty years between them, they continue to discover new things about Boston while researching and writing each edition of this book. They expect to keep looking.